UNECE

Funding and Financing of Transboundary Water Cooperation and Basin Development

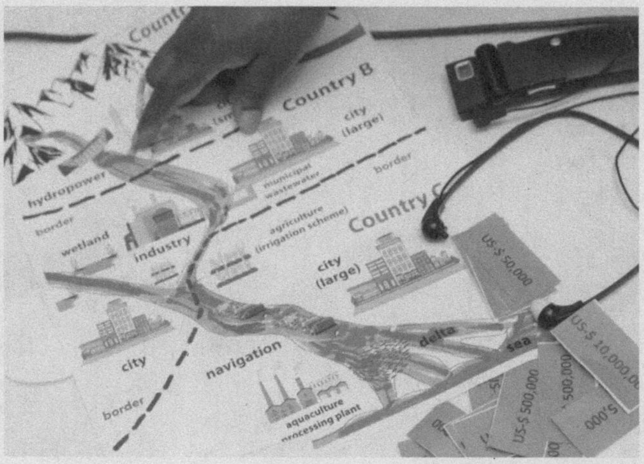

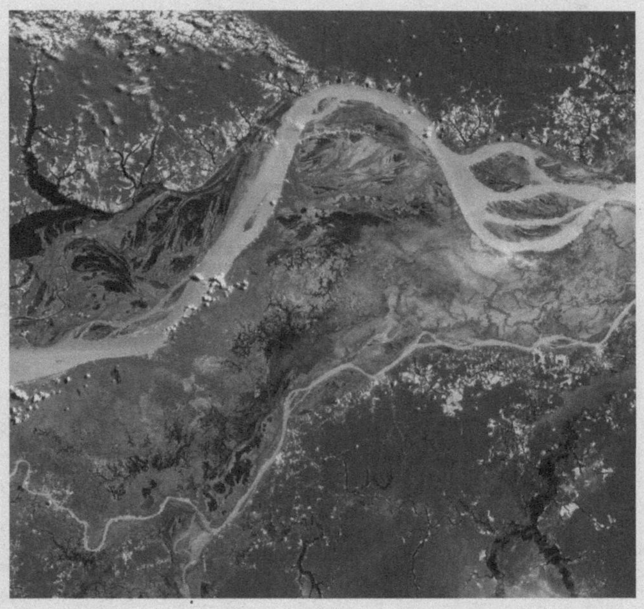

UNITED NATIONS

Geneva, 2021

ECE/MP.WAT/61

UNITED NATIONS PUBLICATION
Sales No. E.21.II.E.7
ISBN: 978-92-1-117270-6
eISBN: 978-92-1-005828-5

Photos for this publication were provided by Kiara Worth from IISD (page 17 and p. 57) and Depositos photo (for all other photos).

Mekong river in the evening

FOREWORD

More than 60 per cent of the world's freshwater is shared between two or more riparian states. The sustainable and cooperative management of these transboundary water resources is crucial for access to water, sustainable development as well as regional stability and peace, as recognized by Sustainable Development Goal SDG 6 (Ensure availability and sustainable management of water and sanitation for all) target 6.5. However, many countries and basins struggle to identify the necessary funding, putting at risk the achievement of the Sustainable Development Goals.

Financial capacity constraints faced by countries as well as limited understanding of the benefits of cooperation often hinder the mobilization of financial resources for transboundary water cooperation and basin development. One of the main challenges lies in the risk perceived in investing in transboundary settings. The Convention on the Protection and Use of Transboundary Watercourses and International Lakes (Water Convention), serviced by the United Nations Economic Commission for Europe (UNECE), helps countries in establishing or strengthening their legal and institutional framework, thereby creating an enabling environment to attract financing, and also supports countries and basins in accessing funding.

This publication analyses the key opportunities and challenges related to the financing of transboundary water cooperation and basin development as well as the different financial needs for the development and operation of joint bodies and basin development projects. It provides a comprehensive overview of funding and financing, including from public and private sources, and innovative financing opportunities.

This publication has been developed in the framework of the Water Convention under the leadership of Switzerland and the Netherlands, and in cooperation with many partners including the African Development Bank (AfDB), the Asian Development Bank (ADB), the European Investment Bank (EIB), the Global Environment Facility (GEF), the Inter-American Development Bank (IDB), and the World Bank. A global workshop on this topic organized in December 2020 provided crucial input and case studies.

We will only be able to address the challenge of financing through broad partnerships, including governments, international financial institutions, international and non-governmental organizations, and the private and financial sector. We hope that this publication will strengthen the dialogue between transboundary experts or basin managers on the one hand and financial actors – both public and private – on the other, thereby increasing the sustainable management of transboundary waters, and contributing to the SDG 6 global acceleration framework and ultimately the well-being of communities around the world.

Ms. Olga Algayerova	*Ms. Patricia Danzi*	*Ms. Barbara Visser*
Under-Secretary-General of the United Nations, Executive Secretary of the United Nations Economic Commission for Europe	*Director General of the Swiss Agency for Development and Cooperation, Switzerland*	*Minister of Infrastructure and Water Management, The Netherlands*

Victoria Falls bridge

ACKNOWLEDGEMENTS

This publication was prepared within the framework of the Water Convention work programme area and is aimed at facilitating the financing of transboundary water cooperation and basin development. The development of this publication would not have been possible without the cooperation, contributions and inputs from experts from several countries and partner organizations.

UNECE would like to thank in particular Ms. Isabella Pagotto from the Swiss Agency for Development and Cooperation (SDC) in Switzerland and Mr. Niels Vlaanderen from the Ministry of Infrastructure and Water Management in the Netherlands, the two lead Party representatives for the work programme area on facilitating the financing of transboundary water cooperation and basin development. They contributed to the conceptual development of the publication and provided technical input and peer review.

The Water Convention secretariat also wishes to thank the following experts for their valuable contributions and comments:

Mr. Ababakar Ndao, Organization for the Development of the Gambia River

Mr. Richard Amalvy, Brazzaville Foundation

Mr. Jelle Beekma, Asian Development Bank

Mr. Edoardo Borgomeo, World Bank

Mr. Francis Daniel Bougaire, African Development Bank

Ms. Patricia Castellarnau, European Investment Bank

Mr. Raúl Muñoz Castillo, Inter-American Development Bank

Mr. Emmanuel Chaponnière, European Investment Bank

Mr. Federico Franco Cordón, Trifinio Trinational Commission

Mr. James Dalton, International Union for Conservation of Nature

Mr. Robert Dessouassi, Volta Basin Authority

Ms. Kathleen Dominique, Organisation for Economic Co-operation and Development

Mr. Ijeoma Emenanjo, African Development Bank

Ms. Judith Enaw, International Commission for the Congo-Oubangui-Sangha Basin

Mr. Mish Hamid, Global Environment Facility IW:LEARN

Mr. Marc Daniel Heintz, International Commission for the Protection of the Rhine

Mr. Evans Kaseke, Zambezi Watercourse Commission

Mr. Tran Minh Khoi, Mekong River Commission

Mr. Péter Kovács, Ministry of Interior, Hungary

Ms. Cate Lamb, Carbon Disclosure Project

Ms. Christina Leb, World Bank

Mr. Jaffer Machano, United Nations Capital Development Fund

Ms. Rukan Manaz, United Nations Capital Development Fund

Mr. Nick Marchesi, European Investment Bank

Mr. Jorge Peña Méndez, Binational Autonomous Authority of Lake Titicaca

Mr. Niokhor Ndour, Ministry of Water and Sanitation, Senegal

Mr. Mamman Nuhu, Lake Chad Basin Commission

Mr. Xaypaseuth Phomsoupha, Partner/S&A Law, Lao PDR

Ms. Biljana Radojevic, Independant Expert

Ms. Gulmira Satymkulova, Water Resources Agency and Chu-Talas Water Management Commission, Kyrgyzstan

Mr. Christian Severin, Global Environment Facility

Mr. Callist Tindimugaya, Ministry of Water and Environment, Uganda

Mr. Aaron Vermeulen, World Wildlife Fund

Ms. Susanne Schmeier and Mr. Wim Verdouw, UNECE consultants, are the main authors of the publication. From UNECE secretariat, Diane Guerrier and Sonja Koeppel coordinated the development of the text. Iulia Trombitcaia, Chantal Demilecamps, Annukka Lipponen, Lucia de Strasser, Hanna Plotnykova, Komlan Sangbana, Sarah Tiefenauer-Linardon, Indira Urazova and Claudio Meza provided valuable inputs and comments. Mayola Lidome and Cammile Marcelo provided administrative support. The publication was edited by Ms. Cathy Lee.

The secretariat gratefully acknowledges the funding provided by Germany, Switzerland, the Netherlands and Sweden, which have enabled the elaboration of this publication.

Aerial view of island on Narew River in sunny day, Poland

CONTENTS

LIST OF BOXES

LIST OF FIGURES

LIST OF MAPS

LIST OF TABLES

ACRONYMS

AF	Adaptation Fund
ADB	Asian Development Bank
AfDB	African Development Bank
AFD	French Development Agency (Agence Française de Développement)
ALT	Binational Autonomous Authority of Lake Titicaca
BEL	Bujagali Energy Limited
CBD	Convention on Biological Diversity
CDM	Clean Development Mechanism
CEMAC	Central African Economic and Monetary Community (Communauté économique et monétaire de l'Afrique centrale)
CICOS	International Commission for the Congo-Oubangui-Sangha Basin (Commission Internationale du Bassin Congo-Oubangui-Sangha)
CIDA	Canadian International Development Agency
CORB	Cubango-Okavango River Basin
CTMS	Comisión Técnica Mixta de Salto Grande
CUFW	Finnish-Russian Commission on the Utilization of Frontier Waters
DEG	Deutsche Investitions- und Entwicklungsgesellschaft (German Investment and Development Society, part of KfW)
DRC	Democratic Republic of the Congo
EAC	East African Community
EIB	European Investment Bank
EPC	Engineering, Procurement and Construction
ERFMNI	Regional School for Vocational Training in Inland Navigation (Ecole Régionale de Formation aux Métiers de la Navigation Intérieure)
EU	European Union
FMO	Dutch Development Bank (Nederlandse Financierings-Maatschappij voor Ontwikkelingslanden)
GCF	Green Climate Fund
GDBWC	German-Dutch Boundary Water Commission
GDP	Gross Domestic Product
GEF	Global Environment Facility
GIZ	German Development Cooperation Agency (Deutsche Gesellschaft für Internationale Zusammenarbeit)
GLC	Great Lakes Commission
GWh	Gigawatt hour
IBWC	International Boundary and Water Commission
ICPDR	International Commission for the Protection of the Danube River
ICPER	International Commission for the Protection of the Elbe
ICPR	International Commission for the Protection of the Rhine
IDA	International Development Association, a member of the World Bank Group
IFC	International Finance Corporation, a member of the World Bank Group
IFI	International Financial Institution
IKI	International Climate Initiative (Die Internationale Klimaschutzinitiative of the German Federal Ministry for the Environment, Nature Conservation and Nuclear Safety)
ISC	International Scheldt Commission
ISRBC	International Sava River Basin Commission
JICA	Japan International Cooperation Agency

KfW	German development bank (Kreditanstalt für Wiederaufbau)
LCBC	Lake Chad Basin Commission
LDCF	Least Developed Countries Fund
LHWP	Lesotho Highlands Water Project
LTA	Lake Tanganyika Authority
LVBC	Lake Victoria Basin Commission
MIGA	Multilateral Investment Guarantee Agency
MRC	Mekong River Commission
MW	Megawatt
NAPA	National Adaptation Programmes of Action
NBA	Niger Basin Authority
NBI	Nile Basin Initiative
NBTF	Nile Basin Trust Fund
NDCs	Nationally Determined Contributions
NT2	Nam Theun 2 Hydropower Project
NTPC	Nam Theun 2 Power Company
OAS	Organization of American States
ODA	Official Development Assistance
OECD	Organisation for Economic Co-operation and Development
OKACOM	Permanent Okavango River Basin Water Commission
OMVG	Organization for the Development of the Gambia River (Organisation pour la mise en valeur du fleuve Gambie)
OMVS	Senegal River Basin Development Organization (L'Organisation pour la mise en valeur du fleuve Sénégal)
ORASECOM	Orange-Senqu River Basin Commission
OSS	Sahara and Sahel Observatory
PIDACC	Programme for Integrated Development and Adaptation to Climate Change in the Niger Basin
PJTC	Permanent Joint Technical Committee
PPA	Power Purchase Agreement
PPP	Public-Private Partnership
PRG	Partial Risk Guarantee
RBO	River Basin Organization
SCCF	The Special Climate Change Fund
SDAGE	Masterplan for Water Development and Management (Schéma Directeur d'Aménagement et de Gestion des Eaux)
SDC	Swiss Agency for Development and Cooperation
SDG	Sustainable Development Goal
SDIP	Sava and Drina Rivers Corridors Integrated Development Program
SPV	Special Purpose Vehicle
TA	Technical Assistance
UNCDF	United Nations Capital Development Fund
UNDP	United Nations Development Programme
UNECE	United Nations Economic Commission for Europe
UNFCCC	United Nations Framework Convention on Climate Change
USAID	United States Agency for International Development
VBA	Volta Basin Authority
WASH	Water, sanitation and hygiene
WFI	Water Funder Initiative
WWF	World Wide Fund for Nature

GLOSSARY

- **Assets:** A resource with economic value that an individual, corporation, or country owns or controls with the expectation that it will provide a future benefit.

- **(transboundary) Basin development:** The development of water resources through activities, projects and infrastructure schemes with the aim of advancing socioeconomic development in the basin.

- **Blended finance:** Blended finance is the strategic use of development finance for the mobilization of additional finance towards sustainable development in developing countries.

- **Bond:** A type of debt instrument, under which the bond issuer/borrower (e.g. a country, municipality, public organization, company) owes the bondholders/lenders (e.g. individuals, institutional investors) a debt and (depending on the terms of the bond) is obliged to pay them interest (the coupon) and to repay the principal at a later date, termed the maturity date. Interest is usually payable at fixed intervals (semiannual, annual, etc.). Bonds can often, but not always, be traded publicly, making them a liquid investment instrument.

- **Credit guarantee:** Promise by a third party to repay debt obligations should the borrower be unable to do so.

- **Debt:** Refers to debt instruments, such as loans and bonds.

- **Debt-to-equity ratio:** Indicates the proportion of equity to debt used to finance a project. This concept is also referred to as gearing or leverage.

- **Demand risk:** Risk created by potential shortfall between forecasted demand and actual demand, for example, in the context of a toll road.

- **Disclosure requirements:** Rules that must be adhered to when submitting disclosure statements in the context of raising capital.

- **Due diligence:** Process undertaken by financiers and others to evaluate the merits of an investment by reviewing relevant financial records, past company performance, forecasts, plus anything else deemed material.

- **Equity:** Equity refers to the residual value of a company or project net of its outstanding debt. As such, it reflects the value of the company for its owners. It also refers to the investment made by equity investors to develop or acquire the project. To compensate equity investors, they are entitled to receive dividends, which are distributions of a company's or project's earnings.

- **Financing:** Funds made available to pay for upfront capital costs that require repayment in the future, typically in addition to some compensation for time and risk (interest payments or dividends).

- **Funding:** Funds made available to pay for upfront capital or ongoing operating costs without a repayment obligation. For example, government grants and user fees (e.g. tolls and electricity tariffs) are considered funding.

- **Grants:** A source of funding, often provided by bilateral donors, multilateral organizations, trust funds and nonprofits. Grants do not have a repayment obligation.

- **Green bonds:** Debt instrument used to finance climate and environmental projects.

- **Impact investing:** Impact investments are made with the intention to generate positive, measurable social and environmental impact alongside a financial return. Impact investments can be made in both emerging and developed markets, and target a range of returns from below market to market rate, depending on investors' strategic goals. Green bonds and social impact bonds are examples of impact investment instruments.

- **Interest rate:** Amount charged, expressed as a percentage of the debt's principal amount, by a lender to a borrower for the use of the borrowed funds. Interest rates can be either fixed or variable.

- **Joint bodies:** Any bilateral or multilateral commission or other appropriate institutional arrangements for cooperation between riparian countries.

- **Loan:** A type of debt instrument under which the loan issuer/borrower (e.g. a country, municipality, public organization, company) owes the holders/lender (e.g. banks) a debt and (depending on the terms of the loan) is obliged to pay them interest and to repay the principal at a later date, termed the maturity date. Individual loans cannot be traded publicly, making them less liquid when compared to bonds. Other key differences with bonds include potentially increased flexibility in terms of the drawing and repayment of the loan, as well as the possibility to negotiate terms directly with the bank.

- **Non-recourse/limited recourse project finance:** Financing structure under which debt is repaid solely from the cash flow generated by the project; lenders do not have recourse to the sponsor's other assets in case the Project Company defaults.

- **Pension funds:** A fund from which pensions are paid, accumulated through contributions from employers and/or employees. Their long-term investment objectives often make infrastructure projects attractive investment opportunities for pension funds.

- **Private financing:** Financing provided by private entities such as commercial banks, insurance companies, corporates and individual investors, as well as International Financial Institutions (IFIs) with a private sector mandate. Note that the latter refers specifically to IFIs financing private sector projects at approximately commercial terms and rates.

- **Private placement:** Sale of bonds or stocks directly through a private offering to a small number of chosen investors (for example pension funds and insurance companies) rather than as part of a public offering.

- **Political risk insurance:** Insurance taken out by financiers to protect against specific political risk, such as transfer restriction (including inconvertibility), expropriation, war and civil disturbance, breach of contract, and non-compliance of financial obligations. Political risk insurance does not cover commercial or technical risks, for which a developer may or may not obtain separate insurance.

- **Risk transfer:** Strategy for risk management, which shifts risk from one party to another in an attempt to assign the risk to the party that can best manage the risk and/or its potential impacts at the lowest cost.

- **River Basin Organization:** An institutionalized form of cooperation based on binding international agreements covering the geographically defined area of an international river or lake basin characterized by principles, norms, rules and governance mechanisms.

- **Social impact bonds:** Debt instrument used to finance projects which augment social and community focused outcomes. Alternatively called "pay-for-success".

- **Special Purpose Vehicle:** Separate legal entity created to develop and finance an infrastructure project. Using a Special Purpose Vehicle construct helps isolate risks associated with a transaction from the parent company, thus protecting investors from liabilities beyond their investment. Similarly, a Special Purpose Vehicle construct helps protect the project and government agency against the risk of default by the parent company. Also called Special Purpose Entity or Project Company.

- **Tax revenue:** Income that is gained by governments through taxation. Governments may impose a variety of taxes, including income tax, corporate tax, capital gains tax, property tax, consumption tax, import tax, etc.

- **Technical assistance:** Targeted support provided to an organization with a development need or problem. It is considered non-financial assistance and can range from information-sharing and expertise to capacity-building.

- **(transboundary) Water cooperation:** Cooperative activities between riparian states with a shared watercourse that arise, and are only possible, because of the transboundary nature of the water resources.

- **Water fund:** Organizations that design and enhance financial and governance mechanisms which unite public, private and civil society stakeholders around a common goal to contribute to water security through nature-based solutions and sustainable watershed management.

Lake Ohrid, between North Macedonia and Albania

EXECUTIVE SUMMARY

The sustainable and cooperative management and development of transboundary water resources is crucial for access to water, economic growth, sustainable development as well as regional stability and peace. The different elements and stages of sustainable and cooperative management, and the development of transboundary water resources, require funding. These elements must be considered when discussing the different prerequisites and requirements for successful transboundary water cooperation and basin development. A lack of financial resources, inadequate funding and/or an absence of financial mechanisms can impede this from occurring even if all riparian states are committed to cooperation and development. The main challenges in funding and financing projects related to transboundary water cooperation and basin development are:

- Water cooperation and development activities and projects, especially in emerging countries and developing countries, are often perceived as particularly risky in a transboundary setting, given that risks normally related to one country (in terms of economic developments, political stability, etc.) are often compounded in basins shared by several countries.

- Many countries face financial capacity constraints and must make tough decisions on how to allocate their scarce public funds. Although this is true for all sectors and initiatives, it is often the case that transboundary water cooperation and basin development is not at the top of countries' priority lists.

- There is often limited consideration of the benefits of cooperation and a general lack of cooperation between riparian states in many of the world's basins, depriving the funding of transboundary basin cooperation and development of its political and institutional basis.

- Most official development assistance (ODA), which could temporarily fill this funding gap, goes to water, sanitation and hygiene (WASH) projects and initiatives, while the majority of international private financing goes to large infrastructure projects that are developed and implemented at the national level.

This publication sets out to explore the different financial needs and opportunities associated with transboundary water management, cooperation and basin development. It aims to provide professionals with a background in water resources management, finance or other related areas of expertise a better understanding of the needs and resources available to sustainably fund transboundary water cooperation and basin development.

The first chapter of the publication provides a comprehensive summary of the financial requirements for transboundary water cooperation and basin development. It differentiates between core costs (the costs associated with establishing and maintaining institutionalized cooperation mechanisms) and programme costs (the costs associated with managing a transboundary basin and developing its water resources and related activities and projects). Both types of costs tend to vary considerably across the world's shared basins, largely depending on the focus and the objectives of cooperation which riparian states have agreed to pursue, and the mandate and the responsibilities assigned to a joint body.

The second chapter of the publication assesses the different sources available to meet the aforementioned financial needs. It arranges them into different categories, namely public funding and financing and private funding and financing, acknowledging that hybrid forms exist between the two and can offer valuable solutions.

On the public funding and financing side, direct member state contributions to transboundary water cooperation, management and basin development are considered, highlighting their great importance for ensuring the long-term financial but also political sustainability of cooperative action. Some of the typical characteristics and challenges associated with these contributions are also assessed. The publication then assesses other, less commonly applied direct public sources, such as regional taxes or user/polluter fees, which come with numerous challenges and have so far not developed into a broad funding base for joint bodies. The publication then reviews the sale of data and services derived from transboundary water cooperation and basin development, as well as management and administration fees/project management that joint bodies can charge for projects and which can provide a source of income, albeit it is not sustainable in the long term. Finally, public funding and financing sources are reviewed and include public loans, grants and technical assistance mechanisms. The publication acknowledges their potential importance for overcoming financial capacity constraints in basins in developing countries and to kick-start cooperation, joint management and basin development, even in times of budget limitations, while also highlighting the challenges related to long-term financial sustainability.

With regards to private funding and financing, the publication first assesses mechanisms of private funding and the role private philanthropies can play. Acknowledging that there is limited potential to meet financial needs in many of the world's basins through philanthropy and other types of private funding, the publication investigates private financing for the development of water-related infrastructure projects. It looks at public private partnerships to explain how they can be structured to achieve efficient risk allocation, while overcoming some of the key challenges associated with infrastructure development. The publication then assesses the role of equity and debt in private financing and how they can be used in transboundary basins. It also highlights some of the constraints related to those instruments, which include a repayment obligation for private debt and a positive risk-adjusted return expectation for equity, making private financing typically more expensive than public financing.

The publication also reviews new developments and opportunities to finance transboundary water projects. These include innovative financing mechanisms and initiatives that have emerged over the past years, especially in the form of green, social impact bonds and blue bonds. The publication details how these mechanisms could work and acknowledges the innovation potential of these approaches; simultaneously, it also informs on the unknowns and the inherent risks of these still evolving mechanisms.

The publication ends with a discussion on funding and financing by exploring "blended financing" as a way to finance transboundary water infrastructure projects, and examines two relevant case studies that successfully employed such an approach. The OECD (2018) defines blended finance as the strategic use of development finance for the mobilization of additional finance towards sustainable development in developing countries. By using public funding and financing, in combination with specific financial instruments to overcome risks that commercial financiers cannot easily absorb, a blended finance approach is able to mobilize private debt and equity financing that may otherwise not have been available. Besides mobilizing additional financial resources, blended finance can efficiently help in allocating risk to the stakeholder best positioned to manage and/or absorb it while potentially reducing the overall cost of capital for the project. Blended financing, therefore, presents significant opportunities to mobilize funds for transboundary water management infrastructure projects.

Throughout the publication, case studies will be leveraged to illustrate different funding and financing mechanisms in action. The case studies describe how these mechanisms were harnessed in transboundary settings. These range from solely public to completely private approaches. Blended financing will be explored more deeply through two longer case studies. Other examples can be found in boxes throughout the report. In this way, the report connects real projects to the various mechanisms, thereby exploring the unique challenges and opportunities that exist under the different scenarios and showing that there is no "one size fits all" solution to transboundary water financing.

The publication then summarizes the key findings with a special focus on the challenges and opportunities of each funding and financing mechanism, highlighting the potential for each mechanism to contribute to the long-term sustainable funding or financing of transboundary water cooperation and basin development, and so that basin managers and others involved in these processes are made aware of the challenges they face.

Finally, the main findings are summarized at the end of the publication in the form of 20 detailed takeaway messages targeted at high-level policy and decision-makers from both the water management and the financial side. The key points of this publication are outlined below:

- It is crucial for states and joint bodies with shared basins to create an enabling environment in order to mobilize financial resources. This can be achieved by building strong legal and institutional frameworks, strengthening governance, and elaborating plans for basin development.

- Despite the challenges related to budget constraints and the political will of member states, domestic budgetary resources from riparian states are and should remain the primary funding source to support joint bodies core costs and basin water management activities. Identifying and communicating the benefits of transboundary water cooperation can help secure these national budgetary contributions.

- To complement domestic budgetary contributions and meet transboundary water cooperation and the financial needs of basin development, a number of other public funding and financing options are available to riparian states and joint bodies.

- Private financing can be leveraged as it offers opportunities to cover transboundary basin infrastructure development costs.

- Innovative financial instruments are being developed and tested. These instruments could potentially offer new opportunities for countries and joint bodies to finance transboundary water cooperation and basin development.

- There is a need for further capacity-building and an exchange of experience and information on the funding and financing of transboundary water cooperation and basin development, as well as on the challenges and lessons learned across basins worldwide.

Based on these findings, water management practitioners, basin managers, representatives of national ministries in charge of economic planning and finances, representatives of joint bodies and international financial institutions, and private financiers can engage in a deeper dialogue on how best to meet the financial needs of transboundary water cooperation and basin development.

Pyandzh-pyan river, Tadjikistan

INTRODUCTION

Transboundary water cooperation and basin development faces tremendous financial needs worldwide. Transboundary watercourses — rivers, lakes and aquifers — are of crucial importance for riparian communities, municipalities/local governments, countries and their entire basins, including for their environmental health, socioeconomic development and political stability. However, the level of financing required for their management, development and protection remain insufficient in most parts of the world. This situation affects more than 40 per cent of the world's population who live near or are impacted by the more than 300 transboundary river and lake basins (and many more aquifers) on the planet.

Map 1. Transboundary river, lake basins and aquifers

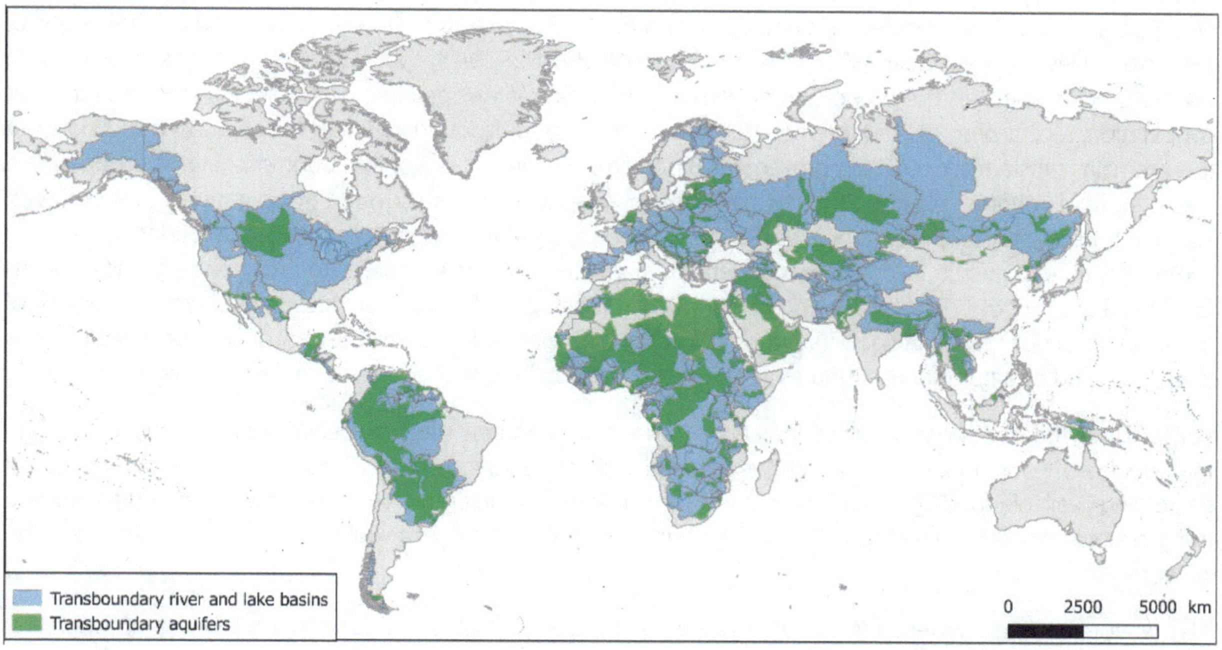

Source: Progress on transboundary water cooperation: global baseline for SDG 6.5.2, 2018, UNECE/UNESCO on behalf of UN-Water

To understand the challenges faced in meeting the financial needs of transboundary water cooperation and basin development, it can be helpful to first look at the challenges associated with water infrastructure development in general. As the OECD (2018) reports, water is often undervalued and accordingly underpriced, resulting in poor cost recovery. In addition, water infrastructure tends to be capital intensive, meaning that it takes a long time to recover those early investments. Furthermore, many of the benefits of water management and infrastructure cannot be easily monetized, thus limiting revenue potential for public and private financiers. Lack of appropriate analytical tools and reliable data may also deter financiers. Moreover, water projects tend to be very context specific, raising transaction costs and potentially limiting the efficient use of emerging innovative financing models. Lastly, by focusing on financial flows rather than economic benefits, financiers and planners will likely prioritize projects with substantial revenue potential while foregoing projects that although may not be a solid business proposition would generate significant positive externalities. In addition to the challenges in monetizing economic benefits, water projects that touch upon multiple sectors often struggle to capture, quantify and communicate the other benefits across all sectors that may include energy, agriculture, pisciculture, navigation and tourism, among others.

All the above equally applies to projects related to transboundary water management and basin development, but there are a number of additional complications that make it particularly challenging to meet the financing needs of such initiatives. Firstly, water cooperation projects and, in particular, investments in them may be perceived as inherently risky, especially in developing countries. Moreover, they are often considered to incur even greater risk when in a transboundary setting given that risks normally related to one country (in terms of economic developments, political stability, etc.) are often compounded in basins shared by several countries. This is particularly true if there is no legal agreement on transboundary water cooperation between the countries. The existence of an enabling environment, including a stable and effective legal and institutional framework, is crucial for any investment.

Global conventions such as the Convention on the Protection and Use of Transboundary Watercourses and International Lakes (Water Convention)[1] may be useful in this regard.

Secondly, many countries face financial capacity constraints and must therefore make tough decisions on how to allocate their scarce public funds. Though this is true for all sectors and initiatives, transboundary water management and basin development is often not at the top of a country's list of priorities. The coordination of water resources uses across countries, the development and maintenance of joint institutions, or the implementation of joint river basin management projects typically do not feature highly in terms of national priorities. Thirdly, most official development assistance (ODA) that could temporarily fill this funding gap goes to the WASH sector, while most international private financing goes to large infrastructure projects that are developed and implemented at the national level. Transboundary water management and development is therefore still largely underfunded despite the growing interest among international donors.

Lastly, another key challenge relates to a limited consideration of the benefits of cooperation and a general lack of cooperation by riparian states in many of the world's basins. According to the second reporting exercise of Sustainable Development Goals (SDG) indicator 6.5.2 (UNECE/UNESCO/UN-Water, 2021)[2], which was undertaken in 2020–2021 and measures the proportion of transboundary basin area operating within an arrangement for water cooperation, recent progress has been made in strengthening transboundary water cooperation worldwide, but there remains substantial need for improvement. Based on data from 101 out of 153 countries sharing transboundary waters, only 24 countries reported that all their transboundary waters were covered by operational arrangements. This also reflects the complex geopolitics behind transboundary water management in certain basins. The limited willingness to engage in transboundary cooperation translates to an unwillingness to provide the financial means for it. Moreover, out of 129 countries reporting on SDG indicator 6.5.2, 76 indicated "resources constraints" as one of the main challenges faced in cooperating on transboundary waters. Moreover, the lack of financial resources has been identified by a number of countries as one of the main challenges they face to implement arrangements.

Consequently, transboundary water cooperation and basin development often lag behind their potential, preventing the benefits of cooperation from being generated and shared across the basin. This can create vicious cycles of decreasing available funding. Failure to manage shared water resources in a cooperative manner and to develop them in a coordinated and sustainable way poses a myriad of threats, some of which have impacts well beyond the water sector.

It is therefore crucial to better understand the needs and sources available to fund transboundary water cooperation and basin development, and to assess them in a comprehensive manner. This can help government officials, basin organizations and other joint bodies, water sector practitioners, and other stakeholders involved in the management and development of shared water resources at various governance levels; it can also assist representatives of donor agencies and the private sector to better understand the mechanisms and processes behind the different funding and financing mechanisms. This would ultimately contribute to a better understanding of and dialogue between the public and private entities involved in funding and financing transboundary water related initiatives and projects, and thus make an important contribution to the sustainable management and development of shared watercourses. In this context, it is also important to acknowledge that the reasons for a lack of available financial resources often lie outside of the financial sector. As previously mentioned, they typically relate to different political priorities or an overall lack of commitment to cooperation over shared water resources, which also helps explain the absence of enabling conditions for cooperation and the insufficient financing.

Previous academic publications as well as policy analyses are very limited. Most analyses focus on the funding of WASH services or water resources management at the national level (Rees *et al.*, 2008; World Water Council, 2015; OECD, 2018). Funding for transboundary water cooperation and basin development has hardly been addressed[3] and research often only focuses on specific topics, such as ODA funding for transboundary water management (ODI, 2002; GTZ, 2007), climate finance (World Bank, 2019), or innovative mechanisms for leveraging public and private financing (Blue Peace, 2018). Additional information for this publication has been gleaned from basin-specific

---

[1]   https://www.unece.org/env/water/text/text.html

[2]   Progress on Transboundary Water Cooperation. Global baseline for SDG indicator 6.5.2 (2021). UNECE, UNESCO, UN-Water. Available at: https://www.unwater.org/publications/progress-on-transboundary-water-cooperation-652-2021-update/

[3]   For some of the few exceptions refer to Henkel *et al.*, 2014; UNECE, 2018, as well as reports that address transboundary cooperation challenges more broadly and which also emphasize the importance of financing transboundary cooperation, such as the Global High-Level Panel on Water and Peace's Report (2017).

documents that River Basin Organizations (RBOs) have developed in the context of reform and financial change processes, as well as from relevant case studies of past transboundary water infrastructure projects. This publication has also been informed by the discussion and exchanges that took place on 16–17 December 2020 during the global workshop on financing transboundary water cooperation and basin development[4] organized by UNECE in cooperation with AfDB, ADB, EIB, GEF, GEF IW:LEARN; IDB, OECD, Senegal, Switzerland, the Netherlands, UNCDF, the World Bank and WWF.

This publication consists of three main parts: Chapter 1 presents the funding needs for transboundary water cooperation and basin development, differentiating between funding requirements for joint bodies in the form of core costs and those needed for the implementation of projects and activities related to basin management and development. Chapter 2 analyses the different sources of public and private funding and financing to cover these different costs. Chapter 3 summarizes the key challenges and opportunities for each of the funding and financing sources, followed by conclusions. The glossary provides an overview of the key terms used in this publication.

---

[4] More information on this workshop is available at: https://unece.org/environmental-policy/water/events/virtual-workshop-financing-transboundary-water-cooperation-and-basin.

Fishing in Salween river, crossing China, Myanmar and Thailand

CHAPTER 1　FUNDING NEEDS FOR TRANSBOUNDARY WATER COOPERATION AND BASIN DEVELOPMENT

Chapter 1 examines the different funding needs for transboundary water cooperation, management and development. It differentiates between the core costs incurred through the mere existence of an institutionalized cooperation mechanism and the programme costs related to the development and implementation of basin management and development activities. It shows that core costs are relatively similar across joint bodies, yet the amount spent on these can vary considerably and is largely determined by the size of the RBO's secretariat; itself determined by the RBO's mandate and functions. Similarly, the greater the implementation mandate of a RBO, the higher its programme costs. Both cost dimensions also change significantly over time, as highlighted by the examples below.

1.1　Core costs of cooperation – through joint bodies and beyond

This section focuses specifically on the costs related to the existence of a joint body for managing a shared basin – often referred to as "core costs," "regular budget", or "corporate services budget". Core costs comprise those that occur due to the mere existence of a joint body and thus include the costs of staff salaries, offices, office materials and other items that ensure the functioning of a joint body, particularly its secretariat. They also include the costs of meetings of the joint body's governing bodies, such as a Council of Ministers or a Meeting of Heads of State, as they ensure the continuous existence and functioning of the organization.

It should be noted here that no clear-cut definitions exist for these terms and they are sometimes used interchangeably, although they may refer to slightly different concepts. In the narrowest sense, the "corporate services budget" can be defined as the budget for administration and services such as finance, information and communications, human resources management (Henkel *et al.*, 2014: 12). Core costs have a similar meaning yet can be slightly broader. A regular budget is broader still and can be defined as the "permanent and recurrent budget that is being allocated or agreed upon by its member countries to sustain the regular basic operations of the institution" (Henkel *et al.*, 2014: 12), which can also include certain project activities if deemed a regular basic operation of the joint body, such as hydrological and environmental monitoring for example. In this publication, the term core costs will be used and understood as comprising the costs incurred for the existence and operation of a joint body, but not the costs relating to the management and development of a basin's water resources. Core costs therefore include:

- Costs of meetings of the RBO's governing bodies, such as ministerial meetings, technical meetings (including preparation, documentation, etc.).

- Staff costs of the secretariat: both permanent and temporary staff as well as consultants who are not part of specific river basin management and development projects.

- Costs of buildings, offices, office equipment, cars and other items required for the physical functioning of the RBO (mainly its secretariat).

- Costs of communication and information dissemination (to member states as well as basin stakeholders).

In this context, it is also important to note that joint bodies come in many shapes and forms. The specific nature of a joint body will also determine the costs associated with it. Generally, one can characterize joint bodies along a continuum that spans from institutions with very limited coordination functions to institutions that have strong implementation competences. The first type – coordination-oriented RBOs (Schmeier, 2013) – are institutions that provide a platform for member states to consult and coordinate water resources management activities, but the activities themselves are implemented by the member states. Typically, these joint bodies have narrow governance structures and small secretariats, or sometimes no permanent secretariats at all. Examples of RBOs with secretariats include the International Commission for the Protection of the Elbe (ICPE) and the Orange-Senqu River Basin Commission (ORASECOM). In contrast, the German-Dutch Boundary Water Commission (GDBWC) and the Permanent Joint Technical Committee (PJTC) for the Kunene River do not have permanent secretariats.

The opposite model – implementation-oriented RBOs – are institutions that do not only provide a platform for coordination, but also have the responsibility to develop and implement projects for river basin management and development themselves. This often comes with broader powers and higher independence vis-à-vis the RBO's member states (Schmeier, 2013: 46). The most prominent examples are L'Organisation pour la mise en valeur du fleuve Sénégal (OMVS), L'Organisation pour la mise en valeur du fleuve Gambie (OMVG) and – to a slightly lesser extent – the Niger Basin Authority (NBA) and the Lake Chad Basin Commission (LCBC). Most RBOs can be found somewhere between these two extremities. Moreover, RBOs can move along this continuum during their lifespan, tending towards a heavier coordination role or towards more active implementation at different times.

The core costs of these different types of joint bodies vary considerably. The core costs of purely coordination-oriented RBOs tend to be the lowest, especially if no permanent secretariat exists. Most of the costs that occur in coordination-oriented RBOs are for staff in the secretariat. The International Commission for the Protection of the Danube River (ICPDR) and the International Commission for the Protection of the Rhine (ICPR), for instance, work with annual budgets with core costs of around US$ 1 million (largely covering staff costs). Implementation-oriented RBOs, on the other hand, tend to have a considerably larger budget, with project or activity costs accounting for the vast majority of all costs[5].

From a cost perspective, joint bodies can make informed decisions when deciding on the scope and functions of their secretariats given certain budget limitations. That is, cost considerations can be a parameter that helps shape an organization's scope and mandate, ensuring that planned activities are also budgeted for in the long term and do not overrun the budgetary capacities of its member states. This requires a careful discussion among member states, but also potentially with external funders, on the functions that countries wish to see performed by the RBO, together with the costs related to those functions. Member states can then decide on the priorities and focus areas of the RBO based on available funding in the near and medium term.

It is important to note that the core costs of an RBO can vary over time and will invariably evolve, especially for nascent or young RBOs. In the first years following the establishment of a RBO, core costs tend to rise as institutionalization progresses, staff positions are filled, and remaining capacity gaps are identified and closed. Once the organization stabilizes, core costs tend to remain stable for longer periods of time, as examples of the ICPDR and the ICPR show.

---

[5] Some implementation-oriented RBOs, however, also have a relatively high share of staff costs despite having a high share of projects costs compared to overall costs. In particular, a continuous increase of staff costs over time might be related to efficiency challenges and may therefore require monitoring and, potentially, change. In the case of the NBA, for instance, staff costs have increased from 62 per cent of the organization's overall costs – a number already relatively high for an implementation-oriented RBOs – to more than 70 per cent in 2008 (NBA, 2009: 43).

A key part of the core costs of a RBO are staff costs. In some RBOs there is a tendency to significantly increase staff costs over time as the secretariat's organigram expands, increasing costs related to staff. The NBA provides an interesting example of this kind of expansion: its staff costs rose from FCFA 302 million (approx. €460,000) in 2004 to FCFA 481 million (€732,000) in 2008 (NBA, 2009: 43), continuing to rise in the following years. This is due to increasing salary costs (staff hires and increases in individual salaries), but also due to an increase in related costs, namely travel and benefits, some of which are associated with an expansion of the organization's activities.

Two additional elements are important to mention. Firstly, the costs are related to the establishment of a joint body as an institutionalized means for transboundary cooperation, and secondly, the costs are related to cooperation that is not institutionalized through a fully fledged joint body but through other (mostly bilateral) mechanisms.

The beginnings of cooperation already have significant cost implications. They start with the exchange, trust-building and negotiations between the riparian states, the setting-up of the required platforms (which allow country representatives to come together in a well-prepared setting), and the actual negotiation and implementation of an international water treaty and, ultimately, the joint body. These costs vary considerably across basins. In many cases in the developing world, third parties have supported negotiation processes, not only by facilitating negotiations but also by providing the financial means to enable these negotiations to take place in the first instance. Examples include the World Bank's involvement in the negotiation of the 1960 Indus Waters Treaty or the support provided by the United Nations Development Programme (UNDP) from 1991 to 1994 in negotiations for the 1995 Mekong Agreement. More recently, GIZ has been instrumental in supporting — and to a large extent, funding — negotiations in the Kunene and the Cuvelai river basins in Southern Africa, leading to the adoption of agreements and the establishment of RBOs.

In some of the world's basins, typically the smaller ones with fewer riparian states (mostly only two states), transboundary water cooperation, management or development are organized without established joint bodies, that is, without a permanent institutionalized cooperation mechanism in the form of a secretariat, for example. Member states meet regularly on a bilateral basis, often in one or other of the states and at its facilities where data and information are exchanged bilaterally without involving a joint body, with projects decided jointly but implemented through the national agencies in each country. Examples include the Finnish – Russian Commission on the Utilization of Frontier Waters (CUFW), the International Boundary and Water Commission (IBWC) between the United States and Mexico, or the Indo-Bangladesh Joint Rivers Commission (IBJC). In this case, there are no core costs of joint bodies. Instead, each country typically has a coordination unit within the ministry responsible for water resources (or a separate entity with such responsibilities). Programme costs for the implementation of jointly agreed activities are then usually borne by each country at the national level, as are the costs of each country's participation in meetings and other activities. This is typically part of the respective ministry's or agency's regular (national level) budget and is often not specifically earmarked for transboundary cooperation, especially if the activities are to be implemented under national water management strategies. For this reason, it is difficult to track specific numbers.

1.2 Project, programme and activity costs

In addition to the existential core costs required to operationalize a joint body or, more generally, for the development and maintenance of cooperation in an institutionalized manner, costs are incurred for designing and implementing river basin management and development activities at the basin level in order to achieve the desired benefits of cooperation. These are typically called "project costs", "programme costs", "activity costs", or in some cases also "investment costs". Programme costs, as they will be referred to in this publication, can include costs relating to:

- River basin monitoring (water quantity, water quality, ecological health, fisheries, socioeconomic factors, etc.), the required equipment, information technology (IT) systems, river basin management software, etc.

- Preparation of strategic plans and related documents (on shared visions, basin management plans, etc.) and processes (stakeholder consultations, etc.).

- Implementation of strategic plans and the specific activities defined in them (including monitoring their implementation).

- Development and implementation of infrastructure projects, especially in the context of basin management and investment plans.

- Management and maintenance of infrastructure projects (if owned and managed by the joint body or any other international entity of the basin states).

Programme costs vary across basins and, if present, RBOs. The magnitude of those costs is largely determined by the nature of coordination or implementation of the RBO. Coordination-oriented RBOs implement less activities themselves, minimizing their cost exposure. Instead, they coordinate the projects and activities implemented by member states. This limits their project costs to the few items that must be carried out at the basin level, such as data and information acquisition, analysis and exchange (including costs for modelling a basin's hydrology or environmental status and related decision-support tools), or for the development of joint basin management plans. Other activities, such as implementing measures to reduce river pollution or to rehabilitate a wetland of transboundary importance, are being implemented by the member states, typically at the subnational level rather than at the national level. Implementation-oriented RBOs, on the other hand, have a considerably higher project budget, especially if implementation includes the development, maintenance and management of large infrastructure projects, such as in the case of the OMVS. The vast majority of RBOs lie somewhere between these extremities.

It should be noted that in the case of coordination-oriented joint bodies that implement jointly agreed activities of basin management and development through national agencies, typically with the involvement of different levels of government, such as provinces/states and local water authorities (Schmeier, 2021), these costs often do not feature at the basin level and are therefore difficult to account for in an aggregate manner[6]. This is even more the case for many of the activities (e.g. the regular monitoring of water quality status) undertaken to meet both national and basin-wide objectives (e.g. national water quality standards as well as basin-wide agreements on a specific state of the basin). For these reasons, it is not possible to provide consolidated detailed accounts of all basin management and development programme costs incurred in the basin.

These programme costs are usually determined by the RBO's management, action or investment plans, which define the activities to be implemented in order to reach specific objectives for the basin with respect to its management and development. In the case of the International Commission of the Congo-Oubangui-Sangha Basin (CICOS), its 2010 Strategic Action Plan called for water resources management that follow a detailed programme of measures to achieve the Masterplan for Water Management and Development (CICOS, 2016). The documents list a number of activities including: pre-feasibility studies of a dam on the Oubangui River that would generate hydropower and improve navigability; the construction of landing sites for boats along the river; and the exploration of eco-tourism opportunities that were to be implemented between 2010–2015 and 2016–2020, which would have provided the budget for the activities, thus determining the project costs of the joint body. In the case of CICOS, the costs for implementing the activities of the SDAGE between 2016 and 2020 were estimated at €25 million. It should be noted that the implementation of these activities has been delayed due to the low recovery of the financial resources set out in the budget and to inadequate financing for the individual projects.

As joint bodies evolve from their early stages, their project costs tend to increase as more activities are implemented under their mandate. A RBO's mandate may even be expanded as it matures. In the case of CICOS, for instance, project expenses increased, albeit in a non-linear way, due to the large arrears incurred by some member states (see also section 2.1), but particularly because CICOS's mandate (originally focused on interior navigation) expanded to include integrated water resources management in 2004. Later in the process, in some cases, RBOs may also reconsider programme costs, especially in light of increasing cost implications, and they may initiate processes to reduce the elevated programme costs, for example, through decentralization.

---

[6]   Accounting for costs at the basin level is further complicated by the fact that costs for the implementation of certain activities occur at different levels in each country – at the national, state, provincial, municipal or local level. In the case of the Elbe River Basin, for instance, costs for the management and development of the Elbe River in the German part of the basin are incurred at the national level, but also at the level of the German states sharing the Elbe River (Bavaria, Saxony, Saxony-Anhalt, Thuringia, Berlin, Brandenburg, Lower Saxony, Mecklenburg-Western Pomerania, Hamburg, Schleswig-Holstein) as well as at the local and municipal level (Schmeier, 2021).

Box 1. MRC decentralization of core river basin management functions

The costs of the Mekong River Commission (MRC) – both core and project costs – have increased since its establishment in 1995. One reason for this continuous increase in project costs was the centralized nature of implementing certain river basin management functions, such as flow and water quality monitoring or the preparation of national plans for basin planning.

In the late 2000s, it became clear that this development was not sustainable, with MRC's increasing budget not matched by member contributions and with donor funding expected to decrease in the foreseeable future. In addition, as member states experienced economic growth and graduated from "developing" country status, capacity advances in member states allowed them to implement river basin management functions in a more decentralized manner. At the 2010 Hua Hin Summit of the Heads of State and governments of MRC member states, it was decided to decentralize a significant part of MRC's river basin management work in the context of a broader organizational reform effort. The ultimate aim of this effort was to ensure the financial self-sustainability of the organization by 2030. In the following years, core river basin management functions (CRBMFs), such as monitoring flow parameters or sediment loads, were identified to ready them for decentralization based on an assessment of member states' technical and financial capacity for implementation. They were subsequently decentralized, with MRC playing a more coordinating role.

While there have been some delays in the process, and not all the CRBMFs identified for decentralization have yet been decentralized (or to the degree that was originally foreseen), this reform has helped to lower MRC's project costs while at the same time strengthening member states' ownership of river basin management.

Sources: MRC, 2014; MRC, 2019*a*

Typical elements of programme costs include the following:

Figure 1. Programme costs of joint bodies

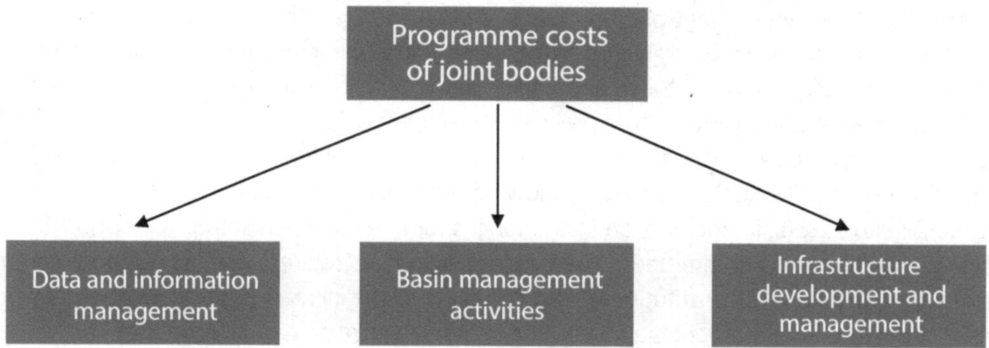

1.2.1   Data and information for basin management and development

Information is required to understand the state of a basin, its significant water management issues, and the changes over time caused by natural fluctuations or by infrastructure. It is necessary for RBOs and riparian countries to make informed basin management and development decisions based on sound knowledge. This requires the establishment and maintenance of monitoring networks for hydrological data collection, the analysis of data in qualified laboratories, the development of basin models, the use of decision-support tools, the production of a "state of the basin" report, the maintenance of a flood early warning system, and/or the assessment of environmental impacts of infrastructure projects, among others. All have related costs, some of which can be significant. The cost of setting up a hydrometeorological monitoring system at minimum functionality, for instance, is estimated by the World Meteorological Organization (WMO) to cost US$ 1.8 million per country. The cost for a "state of the basin" report can amount to US$ 250,000, as was the case for CICOS (in 2015) and the NBI (in 2012), or up to US$ 400,000 in the case of the MRC's latest state of the basin report in 2018. In many cases, riparian states do not have the financial means (or are unwilling to invest in these reports) at the national level, let alone at the transboundary level. Joint bodies have therefore often engaged in data and information management activities and sourced funding for this.

1.2.2 Basin management activities

Basin management projects and programmes also incur various costs. They include the development of a basin management plan and the implementation of various activities identified to achieve the desired state of the basin agreed by the member states. The MRC Basin Development Strategy 2016–2020 (MRC, 2016), for instance, outlines a number of activities such as: a review and update of the design guidance for mainstream dams; the preparation of guidelines for addressing climate change risks including drought impacts; the establishment of a flash flood forecasting system; and the establishment of a regional emergency communication network for floods and droughts, or a study on the potential for conjunctive management of surface and groundwaters (MRC, 2016). Basin management activities often also provide the basis for coordinated basin development, including the development of infrastructure. Funding for such activities is often more difficult to obtain than for the core costs of joint bodies and the more secretarial or data-related functions they fulfil, as the actual implementation of specific activities is often considerably more costly (USAID/CAREC, 2020) than the operational maintenance of a joint body. This holds true in all regions around the world, including in the European Union (EU) despite the general availability of financial resources. Moreover, one of the key bottlenecks for the implementation of the EU Water Framework Directive (EU WFD) remains insufficient funding for the implementation of basin management activities (Zingraff-Hamed *et al.*, 2020).

1.2.3 Infrastructure development and management

Infrastructure projects also require financial resources, from the preparation of projects, including potentially a basin-wide investment plan, to their development, operations and maintenance. Costs for the preparation of infrastructure investments, such as pre-feasibility and feasibility studies, are often underestimated. They can amount to 10–15% of the overall project costs and often need to be borne by actors other than those developing the infrastructure project and who benefit from the return on investment. When joint bodies are already in place and functioning, the preparation of infrastructure projects is often done in the context of comprehensive basin development plans. An example is the Niger Basin Climate Resilience Investment Plan, which aims to coordinate investments in the basin that are most beneficial from a basin-wide management and development perspective, or indeed ZAMCOM's Strategic Plan for the Zambezi Watercourse 2018–2040, which provides the basis for an investment plan that aims to obtain funding for specific activities and projects.

Below the basin-wide level, investment plans can also be prepared by a smaller set of countries in a sub-basin, aimed at leveraging funding for water-related investment projects at this lower level. An example includes the Sio-Malaba-Malakisi (SMM) Basin Investment Plan and Financial Sustainability Strategy prepared jointly by Kenya and Uganda. It consists of eight priority investment projects in water infrastructure, mainly focusing on irrigation, basin management and multi-purpose investments, but also on environmental issues such as wetlands management, as well as a financial sustainability strategy aimed at showing potential donors and investors the value of proposed investments (IUCN *et al.*, 2020). In addition, an institutional structure has been set up to support the investment plan. It consists of a ministerial committee as well as permanent secretariats and an advisory committee. This highlights the importance of sound institutional arrangements and the increasing acknowledgement among basin stakeholders that this structural element is also required in order to attract financial resources.

The development of infrastructure projects typically requires the biggest share of financial resources. Costs differ by sector, type and size of project, project design and many other factors, but in nearly all cases, the costs exceed the financial capacities of individual actors, government agencies or basin organizations. Public and private financing is therefore required in most cases, as discussed in more detail in chapter 2.

The operations and maintenance of infrastructure also needs to be considered when assessing water infrastructure costs. Many countries, whether developing or developed, struggle to appropriately budget for the operations and maintenance of existing water infrastructure (Rozenberg and Fay, 2019). These ongoing costs can vary considerably depending on the type of infrastructure and the selected technological solution, but they are often greater than the upfront investment when considered over the life of the asset. Sufficient and timely operations and maintenance spending in water infrastructure saves further spending down the line; failure to perform routine maintenance increases overall capital replacement costs by at least 60 per cent (Rozenberg and Fay, 2019). In the power sector, another key investment area related to transboundary water management, are annual maintenance costs which range from 0.5 to 6 per cent of the cost of investment needed, largely depending on the technology and installed capacity (Rozenberg and Fay, 2019). Operating and maintenance costs can constitute a significant financial challenge, especially if not planned for properly and/or if no actor finds the management of that specific infrastructure scheme financially attractive. In the Senegal River Basin, for example, the South African infrastructure company, Eksom, was contracted to manage and maintain the Manantali Dam, but when faced with decidedly lower than expected returns it did not renew its contract in 2014 as the project was no longer financially viable for the company. This presented OMVS, the owner of the infrastructure, with a major challenge and a sudden increase in cost. To avoid such situations, it might be necessary to find joint arrangements between countries. This has been done, for instance, in the Chu-Talas River Basin where operation and maintenance costs were included in an agreement between Kazakhstan and Kyrgyzstan on the management of joint dam projects (World Bank, 2018). In this case, downstream Kazakhstan covers the costs of infrastructure maintenance in upstream Kyrgyzstan owing to its stronger economic position. Added to the fact that Kazakhstan is the main beneficiary of the infrastructure; a rare example of cost-sharing measures in a shared basin.

Bridge over the Zambezi river

Wall of the Vanderkloof Dam in the Orange River on the border
of the Free State and Northern Cape Provinces

CHAPTER 2 FUNDING AND FINANCING SOURCES FOR TRANSBOUNDARY WATER COOPERATION AND BASIN DEVELOPMENT

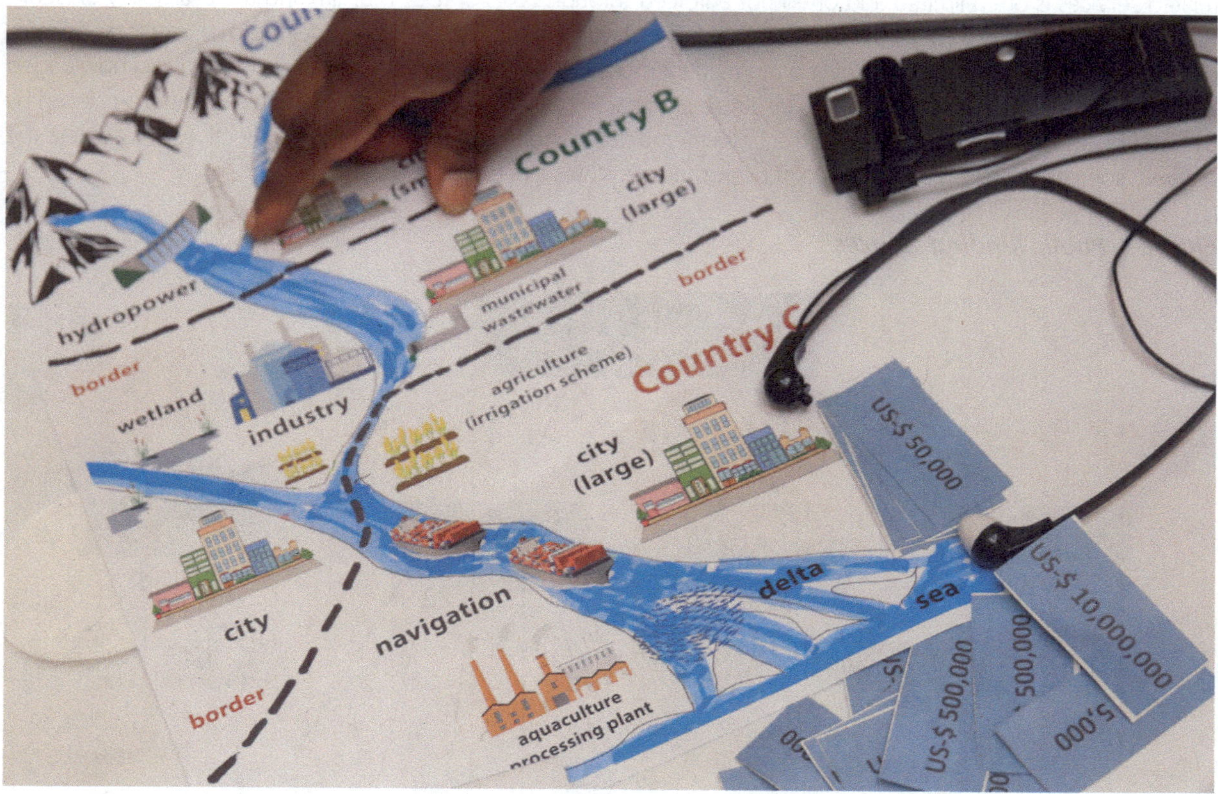

Chapter 2 focuses on the different sources available for funding and financing transboundary water cooperation and basin development. In this publication, funding refers to money made available that does not have a repayment obligation, while financing mechanisms involve a repayment component. In this regard, financing helps bridge the time gap between upfront investment and future repayment, whereas funding, for example in the form of government grants or user fees (tolls, tariffs), is what ultimately pays for projects and activities. These funding and financing sources include both public and private capital at both the domestic and the international level, which will be explored separately in sections 2.1 and 2.2, respectively.

Figure 2. Types of financing sources

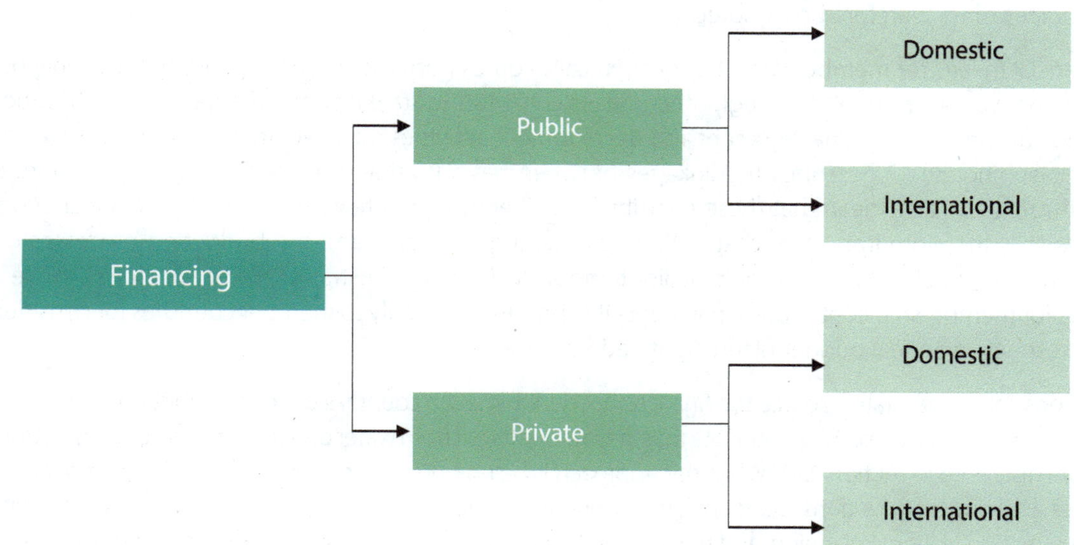

2.1 Public funding and financing

Public funds are critical for transboundary river basin management and development, in large part due to the "public good" nature of water resources and related services. At the same time, the mobilization of public funds has been and still is a challenge, for the reasons discussed earlier in the introduction. The willingness to pay for water resources and related services is often limited and often not enforced through taxes or fees, thus limiting the availability of public funds for transboundary river basin management and development. At the same time, the multi-sectoral benefits of transboundary and cooperative river basin management and development are often insufficiently acknowledged by member states of a joint body, or it is insufficiently clear to them owing to a lack of tangible outputs produced by the joint body, which further decreases the basin members' willingness to pay. The following sections will address the different sources of public funds: from joint body member states to external sources.

Figure 3. Public funding sources

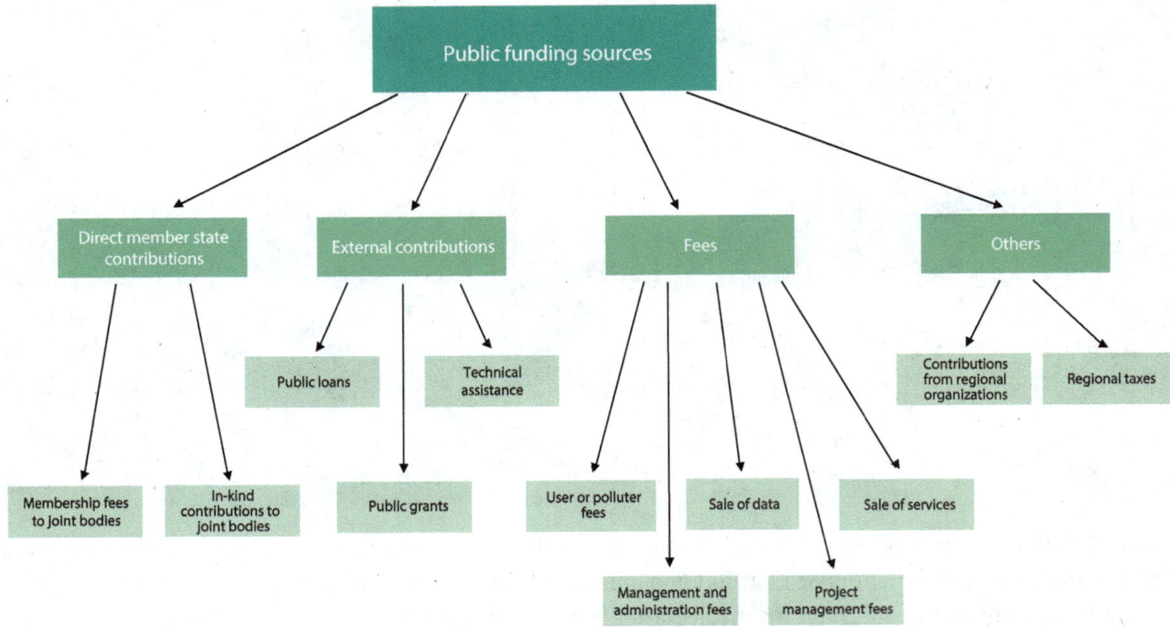

2.1.1 Direct member state contributions

The central sources of funding for river basin management, for both core and project costs, are the direct cash contributions from member states. As previously mentioned, covering the entire budget of a joint body by member contributions is more challenging if the institution's annual budget is high (with implementation-oriented RBOs requiring higher contributions from their members), and/or if the RBO's member states have less financial capacity. Funding only through direct contributions from basin states might then be insufficient and other sources must therefore be explored.

The financial means for member contributions typically comes from the respective country's national budget, sourced from various taxes and through other means constituting state income. The national contribution to a joint body or specific water management and development activities thus becomes an item in a state's annual budget planning. Box 2 describes the linkages between basin level and national budgeting in more detail. These linkages can also mean that these contributions directly compete with many other national budgetary priorities. It is therefore important that national budgeting processes and the budgeting processes of joint bodies are compatible. This would help avoid (temporary) funding constraints that could, for example, delay requests for membership contribution payments if submitted belatedly to member countries for consideration in their respective annual budget planning at national level.

It is also possible to separately source the finances needed to meet a country's direct contribution through specific water taxes, ecological taxes, and so on. Note that these are different from water user fees or polluter-pays instruments, which are discussed in section 2.1.3. While this approach is being pursued at the national and subnational level, no examples are known at the transboundary level. Strong legal, institutional and procedural linkages between basin level cooperation, national planning, and management and budgeting processes are required in both cases.

Box 2. The national level budgeting processes in Hungary

The management and development of transboundary basins plays an important role for Hungary as it shares 24 rivers and smaller surface water bodies with neighbouring countries, including the Danube River; the most international river in the world with a basin shared by 19 riparian states. This is also reflected in well-established funding processes through which the government of Hungary contributes to transboundary basin management and development, and the respective joint bodies set up for this purpose.

For contributions to joint bodies, regular funding is provided through the Ministry of Interior, with the funding for their regional institutions coming from the central government's budget. The Department for River Basin Management and Water Protection is responsible for the allocation of membership fees (to the International Commission for the Protection of the Danube River [ICPDR], World Water Council, etc.), which comes from the ministry's budget, as well as for personnel and other related costs (hosting meetings, cost of translators, etc.) for bi- and multilateral cooperation on water management. There is a specific budget line for membership fees and other voluntary contributions (to UNECE, GWP) and for travel and hosting meetings. Transboundary cooperation activities are mostly carried out through the regional Water Directorates and the General Directorate for Water Management, which have state budget allocations, however, these costs are not earmarked but are built into the general budget. These budget lines provide all the necessary funds for continuous activities. In addition to direct and pre-defined contributions to joint bodies and transboundary river basin management activities nationally, Hungary can also contribute to specific activities and projects of the ICPDR for which another budget can be used. However, as this budget is limited and decreasing, Hungary often contributes in-kind by mainly providing preparatory support, for example, in a water balance project with Serbia under the ICPDR.

This funding is provided by the Ministry of Finance through the general annual budgeting process of the national government. This means that each ministry, including the Ministry of Interior, proposes a budget to the Ministry of Finance, typically in June each year. Once the overall national budget has been approved, including by parliament, a specific amount is allocated to each ministry, usually in September. Within the Ministry of Interior, it is then distributed by the end of each year to the different departments for their required activities, with contributions to joint bodies, such as the ICPDR, coming from a separate budget line.

It is important to note that the budgeting process within joint bodies is closely linked to such processes at the national level. As the ICPDR prepares its budget over a relatively long time frame, member countries, such as Hungary, know well in advance how much they are expected to pay in terms of their specific member contributions and contributions to projects. This means that by December every year, during the ICPDR annual meetings when the request letters for member contributions are issued to member states, Hungary has already gone through its national budget process and can pay its contributions to the ICPDR in January, as required.

Source: Communication with Mr. Péter Kovács, Head of the Department of River Basin Management and Water Protection, Ministry of the Interior, Hungary.

Map 2. Danube River Basin

Source: Encyclopedia Britannica, https://www.britannica.com/place/Danube-River

Another form of member state contributions are in-kind contributions. They can take many different forms, including the offer of a building or office space by the host state, the provision of permanent or seconded national staff, travel costs of government and basin organization officials, or the coverage of other expenses of the joint body or in the context of specific projects. The Government of Botswana, for instance, pays the rented office space for OKACOM (The Permanent Okavango River Basin Water Commission) in Maun and now in Gaborone, while the Government of South Africa provides the offices for ORASECOM (Orange-Senqu River Basin Commission) in Centurion, and grants ORASECOM and its staff certain tax exemptions.

Financial contributions at different governance levels

The main management unit for river basin management and related activities is at the basin level where joint bodies operate. However, there are also coordinated activities implemented at various other governance levels: from the regional/international level, such as the European Union in the context of the EU Water Framework Directive (EU WFD), to the local level through local water management bodies and municipalities (Schmeier, 2021). Financial needs vary at the different levels. At the regional level, regional funds can be used where available; they may stem from regional integration or cooperation organizations such as the EU. At the national level, financial contributions are not only made towards the basin level, in the form of member contributions, but also towards activities implemented at the national level. Depending on the respective government and administrative systems, lower provincial/state, municipal and community levels are also involved in water resources management in transboundary basins, requiring their own financial resources. At the same time, financial resources can also be generated at these levels, for example, through the collection of water use or wastewater charges, which although collected entirely under national authority and thus not directly related to the work of joint bodies, may contribute to the implementation of activities jointly agreed by the various riparian countries in a shared basin. The example of the Elbe River Basin (Box 3) illustrates this point and highlights the funds used at the appropriate level.

Box 3. Funding river basin management across levels in the Elbe River Basin

Similar to other basins in the EU, river basin management activities in the Elbe River Basin take place at various governance levels: from the EU level via the basin level (through the International Commission for the Protection of the Elbe River [ICPER]), the national level (the Czech and German national governments), to the state (namely the *Bundesländer* in Germany) and, finally, the local municipality level.

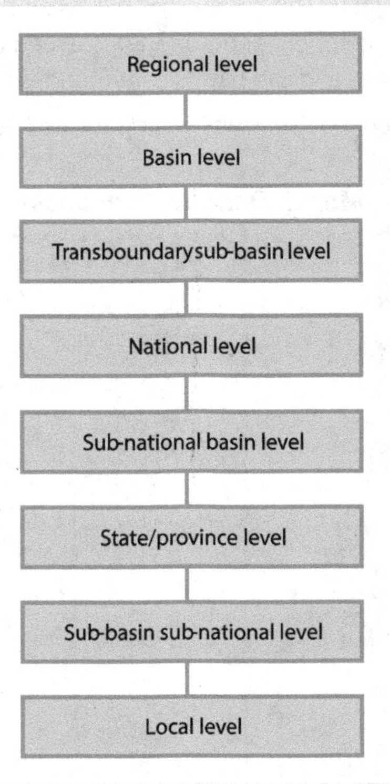

Financial means are both provided and collected at these different levels, yet through very different means. This includes not only the direct contributions of ICPER member states to the joint body to fund the core costs of the organization and its efforts in coordinating basin management activities (funded from the budget of the Federal Ministry for the Environment, Nature Conservation and Nuclear Safety [BMU] that comes out of the national budget of Germany), but also through the funding of activities carried out at the national and subnational (*Bundesländer*) level.

At these national and subnational levels, various national and state ministries contribute to specific activities out of their respective budgets, depending on the specific river basin management activities. All these contributions are drawn from ministerial budgets. Hence, they are ultimately funded through taxes, fees, levies and other sources of government income that are generated at these different governance levels.

It is particularly interesting to note how locally collected financial resources in the form of fees and charges, such as water abstraction charges and wastewater charges, contribute to the implementation of river basin management activities and water quality improvement measures, respectively, as agreed upon at the transboundary level in the framework of the ICPER but implemented at the very local level.

Sources: BMU, 2010; Nolden, 2019; Schmeier, 2021

Reliability of member contributions

The issue of reliability of member state contributions is highly problematic in some of the world's basins. If member states do not pay their agreed contribution, or in a timely manner, arrears accumulate that can place significant pressure on the RBO, which can delay or otherwise impact its work, negatively affecting the projects and activities it is asked to implement. This can ultimately hamper overall river basin management and development effectiveness.

Several RBOs have seen such challenges in the past. In the Niger River Basin, for instance, the Niger Basin Authority (NBA) has struggled with considerable arrears in member country contributions for a long time. Member state contributions fell short of agreed amounts or were paid with significant delays. At the same time, the expenses of the NBA grew considerably, leaving an ever-widening gap between income and expenses, especially in the early and mid-2000s (NBA, 2009). This has led to cash-flow problems in which the NBA Executive Secretariat overspent its bank accounts, as well as delays in the implementation of activities. Development partners have covered some of these gaps, including the funding of some Executive Secretariat staff positions and governance body meetings. The Lake Chad Basin Commission (LCBC) and other joint bodies have encountered similar challenges.

Box 4. Addressing challenges arising from arrears in member contributions (the case of CICOS)

The International Congo Basin Commission (CICOS) has experienced significant financial challenges owing to member states' failure to regularly pay their member contributions. This concerns the Democratic Republic of the Congo (DRC) in particular as it is not part of the Central African Economic and Monetary Community (CEMAC) regional tax financing scheme (see section 2.1.2) and therefore has to pay its contributions to CICOS directly from its national budget. In the period from 2004 to 2018, DRC largely failed to meet its financial commitments to CICOS and made only two payments, representing about 30 per cent of its obligation over that period.

Largely as a result of DRC's failure to meet its financial obligations, CICOS was unable to fill all its staff positions, which in turn led to significant delays in the implementation of activities and an increasing dependency on donor financing. Moreover, failure to deliver planned outputs for both navigation and river basin management and development led to lower levels of commitment to cooperation by member states as the benefits of cooperation had not met members' expectations.

As a consequence of these challenges, CICOS member states and governance bodies are considering to apply enforcement mechanisms in the case of severe arrears as part of its latest organizational reform efforts. According to the 1999 CICOS Agreement (Art. 28), members defaulting repeatedly on their contributions can lose their voting rights in CICOS decision-making processes. While this clause has yet to be applied, it is increasingly being discussed by CICOS member states. In addition, a potential relocation of CICOS Headquarters, currently based in Kinshasa, DRC, has also been discussed as part of its ongoing organizational reform efforts.

Source: IMG Rebel, 2019

Figure 4. Cost-sharing mechanisms

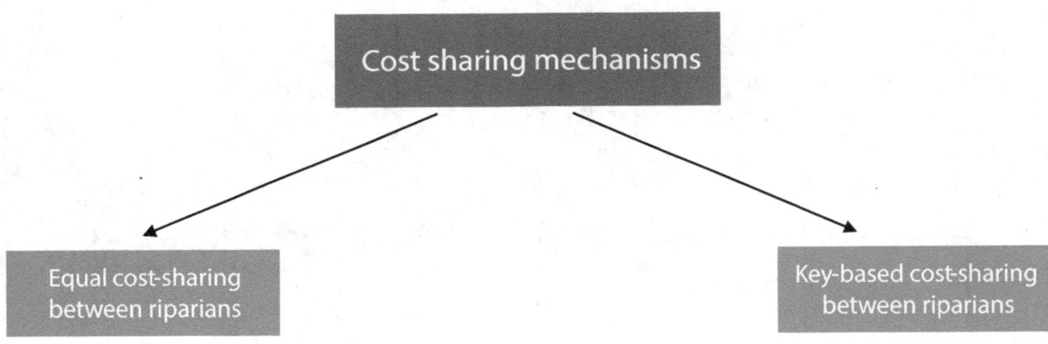

There are a variety of approaches to cost-sharing between member states of a joint body. In a number of basins, costs are shared equally by all member states, that is, each member state of a RBO contributes the same share to the budget. In ORASECOM, for instance, every member country contributes R 500,000 (rand) (approx. US$ 34,000) a year, setting the ORASECOM secretariat's annual budget at R 2,000,000 (approx. US$ 136,200). Once approved by the governing bodies of the joint body, the overall budget will be divided by the number of member states. Other examples of equal cost-sharing include the Lake Tanganyika Authority (LTA) or the International Sava River Basin Commission (ISRBC).

In other basins, differences in economic capacities, shares in the basin, and/or benefits from the basin's resources have led countries to agree to share costs in a non-equal way and instead define certain cost-sharing "keys". Examples of basins with key-based cost-sharing mechanisms include the Congo River Basin with CICOS, the Scheldt River Basin and the International Scheldt Commission (ISC), the Niger River Basin and NBA, or the Volta River Basin with the Volta Basin Authority (VBA). These cost-sharing keys can be based on a number of different parameters (or combinations thereof), including the share of member countries in the overall basin territory and the GDP of the countries concerned. The share of a country in the basin is the most common parameter used. In some cases, the benefits a country receives from the basin's resources are used to calculate a country's contribution in the cost-sharing mechanism. For instance, this is the case in the Comisión Técnica Mixta de Salto Grande (CTM Salto), in which Argentina and Uruguay share the costs based on the hydropower they receive from the joint project. In other cases, contributions of member countries vary depending on the exact budget item to which they contribute. In Lake Titicaca, for example, both Bolivia and Peru contribute equally to the core costs of the Binational Autonomous Authority of Lake Titicaca (ALT), but costs for binational projects are borne at 75 per cent by Peru and only 25 per cent by Bolivia.

There are arguments in favour of both approaches. Ultimately, the specific basin context should guide member states' decisions on how to share costs. However, as a word of caution, it should be mentioned that key-based cost-sharing mechanisms come with a number of challenges, namely, they contradict the principle of sovereign equality that typically guides states' behaviour in international relations. For example, it may imply that countries contributing a larger share of the costs – either because they have a larger share of the basin or because they are more economically dominant — can demand greater influence in basin management and development, which may not always be desirable for all riparian states, especially if they already enjoy a commanding position in the region.

It should also be noted that the manner of cost-sharing can also evolve over time, reflecting changes in the basin or basin states' financial capacities, as highlighted in the two cases below (Box 5 and Box 6).

Box 5. The development of cost-sharing mechanisms in the Mekong River Commission (MRC)

Since the establishment of the MRC in 1995, members' contributions to the core budget have been equally shared among the four member states: Cambodia, Lao PDR, Thailand and Viet Nam (Art 14. of the 1995 Mekong Agreement).

Over time, however, the core budget of the organization has increased and adjustments to member contributions were required to meet the new budgetary requirements. Countries negotiated that these increases in contributions would not be the same for all countries, but would instead be based on a key determined by five factors: the country's share in the catchment area; the country's average flow contribution to the river; the country's irrigated area; the country's population; and the country's GDP. This approach aimed to better reflect the members' capacities as well as the benefits generated from the use of the basin's resources. This led to the adoption of the 2000 decision to annually increase each member state's contributions by 18 per cent for Cambodia and Lao PDR, by 30 per cent for Viet Nam, and by 34 per cent for Thailand.

However, in the context of the MRC's overall organizational reform, the cost-sharing mechanism has been reconsidered in recent years. This was also driven by dissatisfaction of the larger contributors, especially Thailand, over the unequal contributions compared to the benefits gained from cooperation, especially in light of the services and benefits provided by the MRC to each member country. Moreover, concerns arose around the parameters used to determine the cost-sharing key, such as the fact that irrigated areas, but not hydropower benefits, were incorporated. As a result, for the MRC's core budget – estimated at US$ 6.5 million for 2030 – country contributions will again be equally shared.

Sources: MRC, 2000; MRC, 2019*b*

A thorough assessment of member states' financial capacities is also crucial when determining cost-sharing arrangements, while at the same time keeping in mind the implications of non-equal cost-sharing at the political and decision-making level, as demonstrated in box 6.

Overall, member contributions remain very low in quite a few of the world's joint bodies as they have been fixed at low levels compared to the overall budgetary requirements of the joint body and/or because member states have accrued considerable arrears. This has led joint bodies to investigate other sources, which are presented and discussed in the remainder of this section.

Box 6. From key-based to equal cost-sharing in the International Commission for the Protection of the Danube River (ICPDR)

The ICPDR's founding documents stipulate that the costs of the ICPDR are to be shared equally among all member states. At the same time, immediately after the establishment of the RBO, member states acknowledged the tremendous differences in economic capacities across the Danube River Basin; the gap being higher than in any other basin in the world. In order to maintain the principle of sovereign equality, while at the same time allowing all states, including the economically less developed downstream states, to participate in the cooperation process, a temporary cost-sharing key was adopted that grouped member countries into four different categories according to economic capacity. Initially, the countries in the less economically developed categories would pay less and the gap would be covered by the more economically developed upstream countries. This led to a situation where the most economically advanced countries that include Austria, the Czech Republic, Germany, Hungary, Slovakia and Slovenia initially paid the largest share, but shares of the other countries increased over time, starting with Croatia, Serbia, Bulgaria and Romania, followed later by Bosnia-Herzegovina and Ukraine, and Montenegro and Moldova. Over time, however, the former countries' contribution would incrementally rise, and the latter would decrease, until arriving at an equal cost-sharing.

Source: Henkel *et al.,* 2014: 30

2.1.2 Regional taxes

River basin organizations can also be financed through contributions from regional organizations, which may be funded through a type of regional tax such as an import tax. Import tax is typically collected by the member states on behalf of the regional organization, although the exact tax collection arrangement can vary. Tax proceeds are used to support the regional organization's own operations as well as potentially a number of associated specialized organizations and/or projects. Specialized organizations supported by the regional tax may include RBOs. As imports and import tax receipts typically do not fluctuate dramatically from year to year, this source of funding is typically more stable and reliable than direct government contributions coming from the national budget.

The stability provided by regional taxes as a funding source ensures that RBOs can meet their fixed financial obligations while also allowing them to plan more effectively for future capital-intensive projects and to execute projects in its pipeline. By minimizing dependency on direct national funding, the RBO can overcome weaknesses in national budgets and avoid having to compete with numerous domestic funding priorities. In addition, it can potentially avoid being held captive by the interests of the large contributing member states. However, given its role of principal funder, the regional organization could have, or be perceived to have, undue influence over the RBO's work and/or priorities. From here, challenges related to ownership, as well as the specific legal and institutional arrangements for financing, can arise.

A regional tax, although stable, is disconnected from water-based activities pursued by the RBO. On the one hand, the disconnect allows the RBO to act outside of specific national interests or politics and pursue appropriate basin-level activities. It can do this because the regional tax meets basic funding needs regardless of national contributions. On the other hand, as the funding is more or less automatic without any link to the work of the RBO, it may also reduce the interest of national governments as they are not paying for its operations. Furthermore, the RBO cannot set the tax rate, meaning it cannot levy higher taxes to meet funding deficits if other forms of contributions fall short.

Box 7. Supplementing direct contributions with regional taxes (the case of CICOS)

CICOS is a prime example of how regional taxes can help fund RBOs. CICOS is a specialized agency of the Central African Economic and Monetary Community (CEMAC). CICOS benefits from both direct contributions from two of its member states (Democratic Republic of the Congo and Angola) as well as from CEMAC funding, via the CEMAC Community Integration Tax, a set 1% import tax, which covers the contribution of the remaining four member states. Whereas the direct member state contributions have been volatile and insufficient over the past 15 years, as discussed in section 2.1.1, the tax-based CEMAC funding has been relatively stable, thus providing CICOS with a reliable income flow to support its operations and activities. This difference in funding reliability and sufficiency is also borne out in the recovery rate, which was 80% for the tax-based CEMAC funding versus some 30% for direct contributions.

The relationship between CICOS and CEMAC also illustrates the potential complexity of institutional arrangements associated with regional taxes. Not all CEMAC members are part of CICOS, nor are all basin countries members of CICOS and/or CEMAC. As discussed, a lack of direct national ties can lead to less individual government buy-in. In addition, it can create cases of free-riding for basin member countries that are not part of CEMAC and who may fall behind on its direct contributions, as discussed earlier in the case of DRC which controls 70 per cent of the basin but is not a member of CEMAC (Box 4). Although DRC only contributed twice over the past 15 years, and is therefore well behind on its financial obligations, it continues to benefit from many CICOS activities.

Source: IMG Rebel, 2019

2.1.3 User and polluter fees

Considered to be among the more innovative funding mechanisms at the transboundary level, user-pay or polluter-pay funding approaches are based on the idea that those who use or pollute the resource in question should fund the organization in charge of water resource management and/or interior navigation. These approaches have been applied at the national and subnational level in many countries, providing some guidance on their potential application at the transboundary level.

Although in theory all users/polluters could potentially contribute, the issue of transaction cost (i.e. the cost to collect money) makes it more efficient from a financial perspective to target a limited group of large users (e.g. hydropower, large-scale irrigation, navigation, etc.) or polluters (e.g. industry, mines, etc.). However, there are also other considerations that should be taken into consideration when designing a user-pay or polluter-pay system, including cost recovery from beneficiaries, incentives for more rationale water use, and the impact of externalities (in the case of a polluter-pay system).

Under a user fee-based funding mechanism, users are expected to pay for water resources. Large water consumers such as hydroelectricity, irrigation, industry and mining could be asked to pay a charge for the right to withdraw a certain amount of water. Similarly, commercial boats could pay a passage fee. To justify such a system, the RBO or riparian states must be able to provide a clear service or benefit to its users. In the context of transboundary water cooperation, however, it can be difficult for a RBO or riparian states to demonstrate the value of the service. Another potential challenge for user fee-based funding is that member states may decide not to transfer (all) user charge revenues to the RBO. Several transboundary RBOs in developing countries (Mekong River Commission, Niger Basin Authority) considered a user fee-based financing mechanism but experienced conflicts of interest between member states. However, some basins are currently working on setting up such mechanisms, such as current deliberations in the Congo River Basin by CICOS show, which is exploring the establishment of a water user tax for hydropower developers/operators.

Non-transboundary RBOs have been more successful in implementing a user fee-based financing mechanism. Examples include Burkina Faso where large water users, such as mining companies, help support subnational RBOs, as well as in France and the Netherlands where user fee-based financing mechanisms have been used for many decades, generating substantial revenues for their respective organizations. In the case of the Netherlands, the user fee-based revenues are used to not only support the operations of the RBO but also implement specific projects.

Under a polluter fee-based financing mechanism, polluters pay for the damage caused by their pollution. The penalty that polluters pay should somewhat accurately reflect the externalities created by the pollution.

If the penalty is too low, a polluter fee-based structure could create a "right to pollute" without encouraging behavioural change, such as installing water filters if the amount to be paid to compensate for negative externalities is high. If the penalty is set roughly equal to the value of the externalities created by the pollution, a polluter fee-based financing mechanism could generate substantial revenues—potentially beyond the RBO's funding needs. If the penalty is too high, the system could negatively impact the overall economy as beneficial economic activity could be discouraged. If the penalty is set by the RBO and all associated revenues also flow to the RBO, the RBO could ultimately generate revenues beyond its funding needs. A polluter fee-based financing mechanism can therefore only work if the revenues are collected by an independent entity that would also ensure that the penalties are set appropriately. A polluter fee-based financing mechanism also requires that the polluters are able to be identified and monitored through an effective control system, for example, through the use of a "water police".

Although many states have included the idea of user-pay or polluter-pay in their national legislation, there are few examples known where such a funding system generates substantial resources to support water resources management. Different RBOs (for example, the MRC or NBA) have studied the implementation of a user-pay system but ran into conflicts of interest between member states. No RBO is believed to have implemented a polluter-pay system at a transboundary river basin level (Henkel *et al.*, 2014).

2.1.4   Sale of data and services

In recent years, the sale of services has increasingly been perceived as a potential new funding source for transboundary river basin management and development. Various joint bodies, national governments and donor agencies have suggested to sell the regional data collected and processed to other interested parties in order to generate additional income to cover some (typically the core) costs of the joint body (Box 8).

Box 8. The sale of data and services by the MRC

The MRC now sells its data and specific data projects, such as datasets available as CD-ROMS, printed MRC publications or photos of the basin, to users. Differentiating between different user groups (e.g. commercial or educational), prices range between US$3 and US$50 per product or item, plus shipping and data handling costs. The overall income generated from these sales remains extremely low: less than US$500 a year. The sale of data and related services is thus more a cost recovery mechanism, compensating RBO staff for work on extra data and maps, than a promising source of income.

Source: MRC Data Portal

Some joint bodies have also tried to sell services in the form of training sessions or courses or even set up specific training institutes for which they charge education or participation fees, or are planning to do so (Box 9).

Box 9. CICOS Regional School for Vocational Training in Inland Navigation

CICOS maintains its regional school for vocational training in inland navigation, École Régionale de Formation aux Métiers de la Navigation Intérieure (ERFMNI), which trains students from the entire basin in navigation-related jobs (navigation mechanics, sailors, captains, etc.). Students pay a tuition fee to participate in the school's programme (US$ 10 inscription fee per year and US$ 500 per year participation fees/tuition). In addition to these educational programmes, CICOS also offers short-term courses and training to staff of commercial shipping companies in the basin for a course fee, creating additional business for the ERFMNI. In reality, however, little income has been generated on this basis. Tuition fees of more than US$ 100,000 could be generated so far (figures of 2015), but these do not cover the costs of the school (building, costs for student housing, teaching staff, etc.). In fact, income from tuition fees only amount to 14% of the school's overall costs. Also, ERFMNI has struggled to attract short course participants as the financial capacity of many local shipping companies remains low and interest in improved capacities for navigation is limited. As a consequence, the ERFMNI remains financially dependent to a large extent on CICOS and its donors to fund the maintenance and operation of CICOS, and it appears unlikely that it will become a source of additional funding for CICOS in the future.

Source: CICOS, 2015

Overall, the sale of services – whether in the form of data and information or in the form of training or other activities – has so far not proven to be a material source of income for joint bodies. While it might be useful to occasionally review opportunities for the sale of services as a potential additional source of income to fund basin cooperation and development, the associated revenue potential is expected to be limited.

2.1.5 Management and administration fees

RBOs may be able to leverage their role in transboundary water projects to finance their own operation with management and administration fees (covered in this section) and/or project management fees (covered in the next section). These funding sources are dependent on the mandate of the specific RBO; those which are governed by a mandate limited to coordination cannot leverage project management fees and may be constrained to harness management and administration fees. Both management and administration fees and project management fees are challenged in terms of mandate constraints as well as the dependency on fees to outweigh costs.

Management and administration fees are different from project management fees because they are not limited to infrastructure. They are charged on "soft", externally funded non-infrastructure projects or activities whose implementation the RBO's staff are directly involved in. A fee is charged for each payment made or expenditure incurred which is eligible for development partner funding. RBOs such as the MRC have utilized management and administration fees to fund its operating and expenses budget; the fee is based on 11% of the project expenditure. The projects mark this fee as an expense. Effectively, this means that donors co-fund the MRC's operating budget, similar to structures used by international development agencies when implementing projects on behalf of another agency. For the MRC, these fees cover the cost of technical and administrative services rendered to the project.

There is a risk that the staff hours used for the project's management and administration will exceed the fees paid to the RBO, meaning more money is paid out than the fees bring in. This results in negative budget implications for the RBO. It is also possible that these projects, necessary to meet budget needs, will redirect staff hours from more relevant projects to projects that provide the highest income in terms of management and administration fees. This can end up undermining the basic purpose of the RBO as an organization which is to foster regional cooperation and to provide benefits by managing cooperation over shared water resources. It is also important to note that management and administration fees may not be a long-term viable financing option, as the size or number of donor projects in the region declines, so would revenue flows.

2.1.6   Project management fees

Project management fees differ from management and administration fees as they are typically related to infrastructure projects. An RBO may be mandated to perform a variety of activities, for which it can be compensated via a project management fee that may include: initial scoping, negotiating and arranging finance for an infrastructure project; managing feasibility studies; supervising procurement and construction; and even involvement in operations and maintenance. Ultimately, the fee is charged to the owner of the infrastructure, either the state government or a private developer.

Performing these services is achievable if staff members have the necessary skill sets. Tasks that require specialized work may incur additional costs. In all cases, project management fees only serve as a financing mechanism to the extent that the fees exceed the actual incurred cost to the RBO. Again, this option is not available to RBOs with a mandate limited to coordination.

The NBA considered project management fees as one of multiple financing mechanisms proposed to cover its operating costs. NBA member states have, at a policy level, committed to paying for NBA assistance, but this has not yet been significantly implemented. Elsewhere, the NBI uses project management fees to cover its operating costs. A separate trust fund, the Nile Basin Trust Fund (NBTF) and later the Cooperation in International Waters in Africa (CIWA) Trust Fund, set up by the World Bank, transferred funds to NBI for the implementation of project activities; previous work included a basin-wide study to assess power demand and assistance in implementing several hydropower projects. In fiscal year 2018, this made up 23% of the NBI's funding, exceeding member states in-kind contributions (15%) and member states cash contributions (2%), with the remainder coming from a variety of international donors. This system has been effective for the NBI as most activities are recipient-executed.

2.1.7   Public Loans

Loans can potentially help transboundary basins bridge the gap between investing needs now and repayment later. Besides the inherent repayment obligation associated with loans, they typically accrue interest as well. In developing countries, International Financial Institutions (IFIs) can often offer long-term loans at below market/concessional rates to public borrowers and have, moreover, a key role to play in contributing to the development of and the adherence to international water law norms in basins they support. Private borrowers can also borrow from select IFIs such as International Finance Corporation (IFC), Proparco, or the Dutch development bank FMO (Nederlandse Financierings-Maatschappij voor Ontwikkelingslanden), but they typically charge market-based interest rates.

In practice, many RBOs face challenges in securing loans for one of two reasons: i) they lack the legal status that would allow them to take on loans; or ii) they lack a revenue stream that can be used to repay the loan. As such, it is more likely that national governments, rather than the RBO, will apply for concessional loans to be used for large transboundary infrastructure projects. As these loans are entered into by national governments, and typically backed by general taxation revenues, lenders usually assume little to no commercial risk for potential failure of the infrastructure project. An example of this can be seen in the Rusumo Falls hydroelectric project on the Kagera River, which is shared by Burundi, Rwanda and Tanzania. The World Bank lent US$ 113 million to each government as low-interest loans for a total of US$ 340 million in financing. Another example is the Sava and Drina Rivers Corridors Integrated Development Program (SDIP) of the World Bank, which aims to support countries of the basin (Serbia, Bosnia and Herzegovina, and Montenegro) in transboundary water cooperation with a particular emphasis on the water, energy, food and ecosystem nexus, which can provide additional benefits of cooperation if the resources are managed in a more integrated manner. It foresees investments of an estimated US$ 332.4 million for the years 2021 to 2030, mainly in navigation and flood protection for riparian states. The International Sava River Basin Commission (ISRBC) plays a key coordination role and is involved through implementing regional studies as well as hosting the regional implementation unit of the project.

Like grants, loans can come with extensive conditions which must be met in order to obtain the funds. The terms of such loans largely depend on the country's financial situation and past borrowing. In addition to the interest rate and repayment conditions, borrowers must also consider currency fluctuations if revenues to be generated by the project are in a different currency than the issued loan; this is especially relevant for RBOs operating in developing countries with less stable local currencies. Given that repayment is required, loans may be most appropriate for revenue generating activities or projects, although countries can decide to use loan proceeds to fund non-revenue generating transboundary infrastructure or activities. The business case for this scenario is weaker given that the government will not receive any revenues from the project and instead rely solely on taxes or other aspects of its budget to service the loan. The loan becomes, effectively, a country contribution.

Notwithstanding the above, some RBOs, such as the Senegal River Basin Development Organization (OMVS), have received loans directly (Box 10).

Box 10. Public loans for joint projects in the Senegal River Basin

One of the key projects of OMVS, initiated soon after its establishment, was the development of two dams, the Manantali and Diama dams, that were meant to contribute to irrigated agriculture, generate hydropower, enable navigation, stabilize the river's flow to prevent floods and droughts (and salinity intrusion in the case of the Diama Dam), and more generally contribute to socioeconomic development in the basin.

In order to mobilize the financing required for such an ambitious project, a Convention concerning the Financing of Jointly-owned Structures was developed in 1982 that is part of the overall legal framework of the OMVS. It allowed the OMVS to enter into loan agreements on behalf of its member states and to manage financial flows for the projects as well as the projects themselves. Additionally, the OMVS created a special purpose vehicle (SPV) in which all member countries were shareholders. The SPV managed the hydropower structures and the loan given to OMVS. Moreover, a cost-sharing mechanism that defines each country's commitments and liabilities was developed on the basis of the irrigation, energy and navigation benefits that each country would receive from the projects.

Twelve bilateral and multilateral organizations (including national government contributors from Saudi Arabia, Kuwait, the United Arab Emirates and Iran, development banks such as the African Development Bank and the World Bank, as well as expert credit agencies from Germany and Switzerland), provided loans and grants to OMVS to construct the Manantali dam. Specific provisions were given to ensure that each member country made a financing plan to cover their share of the OMVS budget so that the RBO could repay the loan and the member countries would cover cost overruns (in effect a sovereign state guarantee).

Sources: Yu, 2008; Schmeier, 2013

2.1.8   *Public Grants*

RBOs may also have access to grant funds through a variety of sources to complement riparian funding, especially at times and in cases where riparian financial resources are limited or where specific one-off activities need to be undertaken, particularly those with a focus on supporting good practices of international water law and water resources management. These can come from multilateral institutions such as the World Bank, Global Environment Facility (GEF), regional development banks, United Nations, or bilateral institutions such as Agence Française de Développement (AFD) or German Kreditanstalt für Wiederaufbau (KfW). Unlike loans, grants do not require repayment. This makes grants ideal for public agencies who do not have a dedicated revenue stream that can be leveraged to repay debt, cannot take on debt, or whose member countries cannot meet its budgetary needs. Often, grants are blended with other kinds of funding or financing; some grants are conditional on there being other sources to cover the remainder of the budget, such as contributions from member countries.

While grants do not need to be repaid and offer various other benefits, especially for least developed countries and/or countries hit hard by a crisis, such as the current COVID-19 crisis, they typically come with limitations on how the money is spent. For example, grant proceeds are often used to implement specific projects or activities and typically cannot be used for the RBO's day-to-day operational expenditure. Finding grants which the RBO, and the associated project, are qualified for can be difficult. Grants often have a specific sector focus and/or specific conditions. Beyond qualifying for the grant, the RBO must prepare a grant application and often compete against many others to receive the funds. The time necessary for staff members to prepare grant applications can be significant and this can detract from their work on the RBO's regular activities. A vicious cycle may be created in which an RBO that has less money is more reliant on grants, meaning that more staff hours are dedicated to writing grant applications. In the longer term, especially when riparian countries become economically stronger, other funding sources are preferable.

Box 11. GEF-UNDP grants for the implementation of sustainable management activities in Lake Tanganyika

Lake Tanganyika, shared by Burundi, the Democratic Republic of the Congo, Tanzania and Zambia, is facing numerous challenges with regard to shared water resources management and development. The joint management of the lake and its basin is therefore crucial, yet capacities of governments have been relatively limited.

In order to address this, GEF – implemented by UNDP – has supported the four riparian governments since the 1990s with more than US$ 24 million so far. This support was provided in the form of grants to enable the basin states to implement a number of activities, namely, the development of a Transboundary Diagnostic Assessment (TDA) and a Strategic Action Plan (SAP), and to build capacity for the newly established Lake Tanganyika Authority (LTA) that was established in 2008 as a result of earlier project activities.

Source: UNDP-GEF, 2016

Even after qualifying for a grant, the RBO must ensure that it is eligible to receive the funds. Some donors require that the RBO serve as an implementing body such that the funds are used within the conditions set; this excludes RBOs limited to a coordination mandate. Note that these requirements can be different from receiving loans, discussed in the next section. As an example, the Niger Basin Authority (NBA) can sign for grants but cannot sign for loans and payment agreements, which must be approved by member states. In the case of NBI, the NBTF was set up as a separate trust fund by the World Bank and the NBTF Committee as the NBI itself remains without legal personality. The NBTF coordinates donor funds and grant allocations to the NBI.

Another way to acquire and manage grants can be through specific water funds, which are designed to provide funding for basin activities. An example is seen in the Upper Lempa River Basin, which is shared between El Salvador, Guatemala and Honduras. Although not ruled by a joint body, there exists a framework agreement on transboundary activity in the form of a treaty and the corresponding "Trifinio Plan". Using this as a foundation, joint transboundary activities have included hydropower projects and preservation initiatives. Grants through the Inter-American Development Bank (IDB) and regional development banks have funded these activities to date.[7] To support long-term continuity and success, the IDB is currently (as of 2020) spearheading an initiative to create a specific transboundary water fund under the Trifinio Plan. In this regard, last preparatory work is currently being conducted by the IDB together with a research institute in the context of a GEF project to promote water security in the Trifinio, implemented by UNEP and executed by the OAS. User fees and tariffs have also been explored as funding options (Artiga, 2003), but they do not provide funding for transboundary initiatives as yet.

---

[7]   The IDB led the Regional Public Goods (RPG) project in El Salvador, Guatemala and Honduras to develop capacity to better manage the shared resource. This led to a trinational, cross border public policy known as Shared Waters. The GEF Trust Fund initiated a project to better understand the root causes, impacts and gaps related to the environmental threats facing the Lempa River Basin; all three basin countries were involved in this project.

2.1.9 Technical assistance

In addition to loans and grants, development partner support often consists of technical assistance (TA) as part of official development assistance (ODA). Both go hand in hand and often there is no clear separation between financial assistance in the form of loans or grants and TA as they are often implemented by the same donor in a combined manner, making it difficult sometimes to differentiate between the two. TA typically refers to advisory services and capacity development activities for actors in the water sector, such as ministries, subordinate government agencies, basin organizations, among others. The focus of TA is on capacity development, enabling actors in a basin to perform certain tasks, activities and functions in the management and development of transboundary water resources. Infrastructure is less relevant in the context of TA, unless it relates to partners' capacity to plan and manage infrastructure projects or effectively evaluate and mitigate their impacts. The amounts provided to transboundary basins through TA are therefore also significantly lower than the amounts provided through loans or grants, but often still account for significant contributions to RBOs. In the case of CICOS for instance, the GIZ's TA contributions – for a substantial time the only development partner – have ensured the functioning of the RBO and the development of key products, such as the river basin management plan, as well as the maintenance of important services, such as the navigation school. TA thus often plays a key role in the functioning of RBOs.

TA has been on the rise since the 2000s and into the 2010s when various European donors actively engaged in transboundary water management, especially in African basins. In recent years, however, TA support to transboundary water management has again declined. Various bilateral and multilateral donors have reduced or even ceased their support to specific basins and their joint bodies, often in relation to questions concerning the overall effectiveness of these bodies, their financial self-sustainability, or the efficient use of TA funds for fostering regional cooperation objectives, but also due to re-orientations of national foreign policy and development cooperation priorities.

> ## Box 12. GIZ TA support to river basin management and development in the Niger River Basin
>
> The German development cooperation agency GIZ has supported transboundary water cooperation in the Niger River Basin and, in particular, the NBA, over a long period of time, spending more than € 13 million since 2009. In its current phase, the TA project will help the NBA to develop a comprehensive legal framework for transboundary cooperation and to develop and implement a comprehensive planning framework for the basin, with a particular focus on
>
> the water–energy–food security nexus. This support consists of involving technical experts from outside the river basin within the NBA, the provision of short-term consultants for specific, technically complex tasks, such as drafting parts of the Water Charter together with NBA staff and its member countries, as well as the organization of training sessions and workshops for NBA and member country staff.
>
> 
>
>
> *Source:* GIZ, 2020a

It should be noted that the recipients of TA often express a preference to receive financial resources directly, for example, through grants or donations rather than TA. This is a complicated matter as the very nature of TA aims to build technical and human capacities through training, workshops, on-the-job training, the joint implementation of projects, and so on. These objectives may not be achieved through the mere provision of financial resources to a joint body. At the same time, the provision of TA is often related to the secondment or hiring of international technical experts, which tends to come at a significantly higher cost than hiring local staff.

In this context, it is important that the TA provided by bilateral or multilateral donors is directly related to and integrated in the strategic plans and work plans of joint bodies, or the respective member states' plans.

2.1.10 Climate funds

Since the development of the global climate change regime, and in particular Article 4 of the United Nations Framework Convention on Climate Change (UNFCCC), which commits developed countries to financially support both mitigation and adaptation in developing countries, a new source of international financing for climate and environmental purposes has been developed: international climate funds. While often mentioned in the context of development cooperation (World Bank, 2019), these funds are different insofar as they arise from a climate-specific treaty obligation entered into by developed countries under the framework of the climate change regime. Nonetheless, there are considerable similarities to international development financing. This section provides an overview of some of the existing climate funds, without attempting to cover all the funds. The main focus is to highlight the opportunities and challenges related to the use of these funds for transboundary water management and basin development.

Green Climate Fund

The Green Climate Fund (GCF) became fully operational in 2015, which was followed by the signing of the Paris Agreement in 2016, with the goal to fund activities related to adaptation and mitigation in the context of developing countries Nationally Determined Contributions (NDCs) by financing the incremental costs related to climate change. Access to the GCF requires countries to collaborate with GCF-accredited agencies. For regional projects, support from all countries involved need to be proven to the GCF.

Despite its very appealing nature, experiences with GCF funding by regional organizations including joint bodies, are still limited. The Sahara and Sahél Observatory (OSS) successfully undertook the accreditation process with GCF in 2017, allowing it to prepare project proposals for GCF financing. Based on the specific type of accreditation that OSS received, it can apply for GCF funding up to US$10 million. So far, concept notes for potential projects, many of which concern regional matters other than water, have been developed, but final project development and the decision on funding is still pending. Another example is the NBA that mobilized GCF funding among other financial sources for its Programme for Integrated Development and Adaptation to Climate Change in the Niger Basin (PIDAAC), which was established from the actions identified in its Climate Resilience Investment Plan (CRIP) (Box 13).

Box 13. The Niger Basin: first transboundary basin to receive GCF funding for a transboundary climate change adaptation project

The Niger Basin is home to more than 112 million people across Benin, Burkina Faso, Cameroon, Chad, Côte d'Ivoire, Guinea, Mali, Niger and Nigeria. The Niger River provides drinking water, irrigation, aquaculture, energy and transport to these nine riparian countries. Climate variability has long been a challenge and an obstacle for development in the basin. Developed in 2015, the Climate Resilience Investment Plan (CRIP) has formed the basis of the Programme for Integrated Development and Adaptation to Climate Change in the Niger Basin (PIDACC). Elaborated by the NBA and its member countries, its objective is to address the effect of climate change in the Niger River Basin including by strengthening the shared management of its natural resources. Following several years of cooperation and discussion with financial partners, the GCF finally approved funding for the PIDACC through the African Development Bank, making the Niger basin the first transboundary basin to receive financial support from the GCF for a transboundary project. The success of the NBA in approaching financial partners and securing funding for the PIDACC is related to the political will of the member states to cooperate, demonstrated by the co-funding from the NBA member states. The existence of a solid shared investment plan developed for the basin was also key in the process as it was coherent with long-term development objectives. Finally, the implications of other financiers in the project, such as AfDB, the GEF, KfW, the European Union and the World Bank, was also crucial.

Source: Presentation of the Development and financing of Niger basin's climate resilience investment plan, NBA Executive Secretary, Mr. Abderahim Bireme Hamid, COP 24, December 2018

Adaptation Fund

The Adaptation Fund (AF) was established in 2001 and officially launched in 2007 in the context of the Kyoto Protocol to support developing countries in coping with the effects of climate change. It has been increasingly active in recent years in supporting projects at the regional level or with a regional focus, involving joint bodies and other regional organizations. The AF is financed through the Kyoto Protocol Clean Development Mechanism (CDM), which generates funding for projects in developing countries through emission reduction projects and emission trading schemes between developed and developing countries. The AF is managed by the GEF and can be accessed by any country that has established a dedicated and accredited national implementing entity. This allows access to funds without going through specific implementing agencies normally involved in GEF projects, such as the World Bank or UNDP. AF is explicitly open for regional and transboundary projects; neighbouring countries that share similar adaptation challenges can jointly apply if their national implementing agencies partner together and if they can prove the added value of a regional approach.

Box 14. The Lake Victoria Basin Commission (LVBC) funding from the Adaptation Fund

The Lake Victoria Basin and the Lake Victoria Basin Commission (LVBC) have been among the first to benefit from AF funding. Based on earlier studies on climate vulnerability assessments and climate change adaptation strategy for the basin undertaken by LVBC's parent organization, the East African Community (EAC), LVBC proposed a project for implementing these strategies, which was accepted by the AF in 2017 and ran from 2018 to 2020.

The project is implemented by UNEP as the EAC is not accredited with the GCF (World Bank, 2019: 18, LVBC, 2019). It focuses on reducing vulnerability to the negative effects of climate change in basin countries, and provides US$ 5 million to LVBC as the executing agency. Activities include: strengthening institutional and technical capacity to integrate climate resilience into transboundary water management; the improvement of climate information and its availability to policymakers, technical experts and local communities; and specific projects with local communities.

Source: GCF, 2020

The OSS has also been accredited with the AF since 2013. On this basis, a national water project in Uganda was prepared as the first OSS AF project shortly after accreditation. Two regional projects followed a few years later: the 2019 project, "Integration of climate change adaptation measures in the consolidated management of the transboundary WAP (ADAPT-WAP) Complex", which benefits Benin, Burkina Faso and Niger and, in particular, a transboundary biosphere reserve and two parks in these countries with the aim to strengthen ecosystem resilience against climate-related threats such as floods, droughts and bush fires; and the 2020 project, "Strengthening Drought Resilience of Small Farmers and Pastoralists in the IGAD Region (DRESS-EA)", which covers Djibouti, Kenya, Uganda and Sudan and aims to increase the resilience of small farmers and pastoralists to drought by developing early warning systems and by implementing adaptation actions. Another proposal is currently being prepared that focuses on drought resilience for local communities in South West Africa.

A third case of AF financing for transboundary water management can be found in the Drin River Basin project, "Integrated Climate-resilient Transboundary Flood Risk Management in the Drin River Basin in the Western Balkans (Drin FRM)", which was approved in 2019. This project builds on earlier activities by other donors and focuses on the flood resilience dimension of the Drin River Basin Strategic Action Plan (SAP) developed in previous years. It is implemented by UNDP, similar to the case outlined earlier (Box 14) on the LVBC.

Another example of successful AF financing can be found in the Volta River Basin. In partnership with the Global Water Partnership (GWP), among others, the Volta Basin Authority (VBA) successfully acquired a project amounting to US$ 7.9 million to support flood and drought management covering the period 2019 to 2023. Common to other basins and AF-funded projects, the VBA also encountered challenges in acquiring and implementing the project, which can provide important lessons to other joint bodies intending to engage in this type of funding. These include the coordination between the different actors involved in the project (the joint body was required to team up with other actors in applying for the funds); a challenge that is certainly not unique to climate fund funding but seems to be particularly complex for many of the climate fund projects in terms of set-ups and structures.

Other global climate funds

Smaller climate funds have also been set up for specific groups of countries or sectors. The Special Climate Change Fund (SCCF), for example, provides support to adaptation projects in developing countries in specific sectors, including water management, and is open to all developing countries that are parties to the UNFCCC. The Least Developed Countries Fund (LDCF) supports the preparation of National Adaptation Programmes of Action (NAPAs) in least developed countries. Both funds are managed by GEF. They have so far not supported any transboundary water management or development projects nor engaged with any RBO.

Experiences of joint bodies with climate funds are still limited. Overall, the situation to date shows that accessing these funds for transboundary water management is not easy for various reasons. To begin with, transboundary water management does not rank high on the priority lists of these funds. This is because the transboundary water management community has so far – in spite of the obvious linkages between the hydrological cycle and climate change – struggled to highlight the specific benefits of transboundary projects for climate change adaptation, or shown the additional value of these projects compared to more traditional development financing through loans and grants instead of climate funds. In addition, data on climate change to support the articulation of a climate rationale is often lacking, especially in least developed countries and their basins, while short-term development needs seem more pressing than long-term climate measures.

Furthermore, it largely remains unclear whether and how regional entities and intergovernmental organizations – such as RBOs – can access these funds directly if at all, and if so, under what conditions. In this context, it is important to note that some funds, such as GCF, do not always cover the full costs of a project. This means that the joint body would need to raise the remaining funds from its member states, which often lack these financial capacities, or from other sources, namely donors, as was the case for the NBA in the financing of the PIDACC.

To conclude, for RBOs to access such funding schemes, they must endure highly complicated and considerably varied processes and procedures across funds. As is the case with other types of grants discussed in section 2.1.8, the technical, human and financial capacity of joint bodies to prepare proposals and engage in the often very long and complicated application processes is, however, limited. Unfortunately, this is particularly true for joint bodies in developing regions that need financial resources the most, in order to fulfil their important role in coordinating climate change adaptation measures of riparian states and to engage in joint activities such as the development of basin-wide vulnerability assessments, but have the least capacity. RBOs struggle with so many different challenges, requirements and tasks that expecting them to effectively fulfil this role of basin-wide coordinators and implementers of climate change adaptation measures may be slightly unrealistic and will depend on the budget, mandate, financial structure and human resources of the respective joint body. Member states providing expertise to their RBOs through relevant ministries and government agencies that handle climate finance matters at the national level might be a promising way to bridge these gaps, although it is not always possible, especially in least developed countries. Moreover, it requires a considerable commitment from member states to their RBOs and to joint, cooperative and trustful basin management and development.

Box 15. IKI support to wetlands management in the Nile River Basin

The German IKI mechanism provides funding of €6 million (2015–2021) to the Nile Basin Initiative (NBI) and its member states to strengthen its technical and institutional capacities for sustainably managing wetlands in the Nile River Basin as a means for climate change adaptation.

The project produced several important analytical tools and studies, including an assessment of the economic dimensions of wetlands, the role of peatlands in the basin for greenhouse gas storage and thus climate change mitigation, as well as an inventory of regionally important wetlands and their ecological status. The project also helped analyse the environmental flow needs in the Nile River Basin that feed into the NBI basin planning process aimed at integrating wetland needs into basin-wide planning, and at developing specific wetland management plans that can help adapt to climate change through green storage, flood protection, and so on.

The project is implemented by the NBI.

Sources: GIZ, 2020b; IKI, 2020

National climate funds

In addition to these global efforts, some developed countries have set up their own climate funds to implement their specific goals. The set-ups, focus areas and types of projects funded vary considerably. For instance, the International Climate Initiative (IKI), established in 2008 by the German Federal Ministry for the Environment, Nature Conservation and Nuclear Safety (BMU), helps implement Germany's commitments under the UNFCCC and the Convention on Biological Diversity (CBD). Support is provided to activities in developing countries that are determined in these countries' NDCs, including measures on climate change adaptation in the water sector. The selection of projects is conducted through a competitive 2-step process based on a country-specific or a theme-specific call that is issued regularly. So far, IKI has committed more than € 3.9 billion (2008–2019) for more than 730 climate-related projects. These include projects focused on transboundary water resources in the Congo, Mekong, the Mono and Nile river basins with regard to climate change scenarios and their impact on tropical forests, climate-smart flood protection, transboundary biodiversity protection, and wetlands management, respectively.

2.2   Private funding and financing

In addition to public funding and financing, there is potential to leverage private capital in transboundary water cooperation and basin development, which is typically limited to infrastructure projects. Although private capital comes largely in the form of debt or equity financing, there is a limited number of examples of private funding in the form of donations and grants.

In this context, it is interesting to note that a growing number of private investors are taking into account sustainability criteria. As shareholders' interests in and commitment to sustainability grows, large investors, such as investment funds or pension funds, are increasingly considering such criteria. This is often done with the support of advisory companies or not-for-profit organizations that monitor investment risks, as well as investment criteria relating to sustainability, which is increasingly used. While transboundary considerations such as compliance with international water law principles, the obligation to prevent significant harm, or the involvement of a joint body in a shared basin are not yet part of investment criteria, there seems to be a global trend towards sustainable investments that benefit shared basins and the institutions that manage and develop them.

A specific approach is the "People-First PPP Evaluation Methodology for the SDGs" (UNECE, 2021), which was developed by the UNECE. This mechanism aims to evaluate infrastructure projects, especially those funded through Public-Private Partnerships (PPPs), with regard to the benefits accrued on behalf of· the riparian communities, i.e. the intended main beneficiaries of the projects. Its five desirable outcomes: access and equality; environmental sustainability; economic effectiveness; replicability; and stakeholder engagement, are also applicable to infrastructure projects in transboundary basins.

2.2.1   Private funding

It should be stressed that private philanthropies and donations to RBOs and basin member states without any repayment obligation or return expectation are rare. Examples mostly arise in the face of disasters when private citizens indirectly donate to RBOs to support recovery efforts from floods or similar events. This includes the US$5.5 billion in private donations received in response to the 2004 Indian Ocean earthquake and tsunami. The funds were largely disbursed to non-profit organizations which funnelled a portion of the funds to transboundary water projects as well as recovery and reconstruction efforts.[8] The Great Lakes Commission (Box 16) is another example of the private funding of a RBO.

Box 16. Great Lakes Commission – Private Funding in Action

The Great Lakes Commission (GLC) is a transboundary RBO created through an interstate pact. A significant portion of its budget comes through private philanthropy. In many ways, GLC operates as a non-profit organization despite being an RBO. The Charles Stewart Mott Foundation, the Joyce Foundation, and the Erb Family Foundation form the core of the GLC donor base. Transboundary project work is directly billable to the various foundations, while operations and baseline budget is covered by state funds. As private funding is such a sizable part of the budget, GLC must be flexible as the foundations' priorities, and thus funding, shift from year to year.

Source: Interview with former GLC staff

---

[8]   The funds were channeled through the EU, World Bank and UNDP under a tripartite agreement that mobilized RBOs to help with recovery and reconstruction plans. Based on the documents available, it cannot be determined who were the actual beneficiaries of the funds.

Some new and promising initiatives are, however, developing that highlight an increasing interest in private philanthropies in transboundary water issues as well as a growing acknowledgment by funders of the need to act in a coordinated manner. The Water Funder Initiative, for instance, is a coalition of family foundations that provide philanthropic funding to various causes whose aim is to identify and fund promising water solutions. This includes a commitment to basin level management in order to balance environmental, social and economic considerations (Earth Security Partnerships, 2018).

Overall, it is important to note that such private philanthropic contributions will only be able to cover certain activities, such as specific projects that are notably of great public interest and are particularly attractive, but they will not replace, nor should they attempt to replace, public funding for transboundary water management and basin development.

2.2.2   Private financing

As private funding in transboundary water cooperation and basin development is rare, the remainder of this chapter will focus on private financing of infrastructure projects. In this context, private financing in the form of debt and equity refers to investments made by private entities in public sector projects. These investments are expected to not only be repaid, but also generate positive returns. Depending on the type of private finance used, these returns could be in the form of interest on debt or dividends on equity. The actors can be commercial banks, private companies, entrepreneurs or investment funds, among others. Table 1 provides an overview of the most relevant instruments available for private financing of transboundary water infrastructure projects as well as potential investor groups for each.

Table 1. Types of private financing instruments

Category	Instrument	Examples of potential investors/providers
Debt	Bank loans	• Domestic and international commercial banks • International financial institutions with private sector mandate
	Bonds	• Retail bond investors • Investment funds
	Private placements	• Pension funds • Insurance companies
Equity		• Domestic and international entrepreneurs/corporates, including construction companies and utilities • Infrastructure development funds • International financial institutions with private sector mandate and ability to invest equity
Credit Guarantees and Political Risk Insurance		• International financial institutions • Export credit agencies

Private financing comes with a myriad of risks and challenges. For this reason, it is not heavily utilized for transboundary water cooperation and basin development with issues that include the need to repay the investment principal and to generate a positive risk-adjusted return, as reflected in the interest rate (for debt) and internal rate of return (for equity). This requires a reliable and sufficiently large revenue stream, which may not always be available. Compounding the problem of revenue generation is the social belief that water is a free public good. This may reduce consumer willingness to pay, thus complicating the monetization of (often intangible) water management benefits and limiting revenue generation potential.

Debt: Debt refers to loans or bonds, which need to be repaid over time. To compensate lenders, they receive interest on the outstanding debt balance. In addition, they may receive certain financing fees.

Equity: Equity refers to the value of a company or project net of its outstanding debt. As such, it reflects the value for its owners. It also refers to the investment made by equity investors to develop or acquire the project. To compensate equity investors, they are entitled to receive dividends, which are distributions of a company's or project's earnings.

Another issue is the complex environment found in transboundary basins. Numerous stakeholders operating in different sectors and countries, with potentially different enabling environments with regard to hydrological, environmental, economic, social or political conditions, must coordinate and cooperate. Furthermore, depending on the geographical location, there may be a higher (perceived) risk of political instability, which either increases the cost of private capital or makes private capital unavailable altogether. Currency risks can further complicate private financing as lenders are typically reluctant to take on currency risk. This is particularly relevant if local debt markets are insufficient and foreign currency must be used. In this context, transboundary projects which span multiple currency regimes are especially vulnerable. All these issues are in addition to the typical complexities that come with implementing large infrastructure projects in potentially remote locations.

These considerations constrain the availability of private capital for water management. Notwithstanding these challenges, private capital has been leveraged to develop transboundary water management infrastructure projects, typically through a PPP approach for revenue generating assets, even though a similar structure can be used for non-revenue generating assets. Before discussing how private debt and equity can be used to develop transboundary water infrastructure projects, the following section provides a basic understanding of PPPs and how they work.

Defining public-private partnerships (PPPs)

PPPs are a financing form that is situated between full *public* ownership and operation/maintenance of the assets and full *private* ownership and operation/maintenance of the assets. It aims to harvest benefits by combining public and private engagement and the added values each side can bring to the table. PPPs can take many forms and often can mean different things to different people. In the context of this publication, PPPs will refer to a long-term agreement (the Project Agreement) between a public and private entity to provide a public asset. Although different models exist, the private entity (often referred to as the Project Company) will typically be responsible for the design, construction, operations, maintenance and financing of the asset. The Project Agreement defines the exact rights and responsibilities of both the Project Company and the public entity, and thus lays the legal and operational framework for collaboration between those for project development and implementation. The Project Company often consists of a developer as well as multiple subcontractors, each subcontracted to play a part within the project's scope, for example, in terms of design, civil works, operations or maintenance.

Many of the risks associated with the design, construction and operation of the asset are typically allocated to the Project Company, with the public entity retaining substantially less risk than under a purely public project. At the end of the Project Agreement, the asset is transferred back to the public entity in a condition that satisfies the requirements outlined in the Project Agreement, often at no cost to the public entity. The long term and integrated nature of the Project Agreement incentivizes the Project Company to maximize innovation and incorporate operations and maintenance considerations into its design, thus reducing the overall lifecycle cost of the asset. In addition, more efficient risk management can further reduce costs. A simplified overview of the contractual structure of a typical PPP project is shown in figure 5.

Figure 5. Typical PPP structure

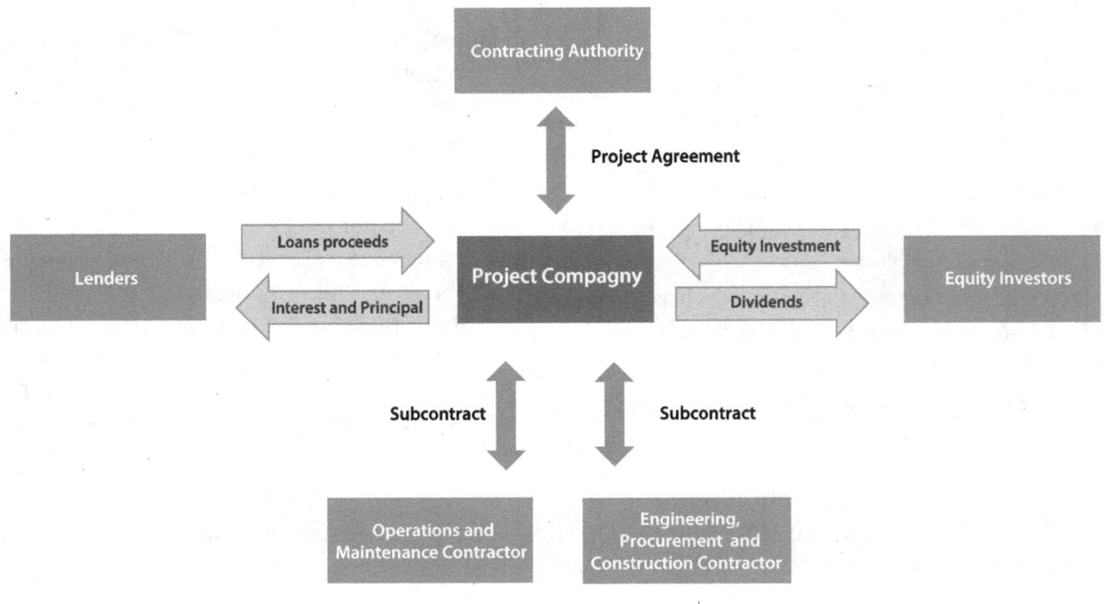

To raise private debt and equity, a non-recourse or limited recourse project finance structure is usually employed. Under this structure, debt and equity are repaid from the cash flow generated by the project. Lenders only have recourse to the project's revenues and assets in case the Project Company defaults. This structure allows for a highly customized, and therefore efficient, financing structure that reflects the project's risk profile and risk allocation among the different parties involved. Depending on the type of infrastructure being developed, different payment mechanisms to compensate the Project Company for its investments can be used, including performance-based availability payments and user fees (tariffs, tolls, etc.). In developing markets, PPPs have more often been used for revenue generating assets as non-revenue generating assets create additional government liabilities that would need to be repaid through taxation. A project-specific deduction or penalty regime as defined in the Project Agreement can help ensure performance throughout the life of the project.

The payment mechanism for energy generating facilities, such as hydropower plants, is typically tied directly to the amount of electricity produced, whereas developing a payment mechanism for a multipurpose water infrastructure PPP project may be more challenging. For example, the payment mechanism for a multipurpose dam that is used for electricity production, river regulation, irrigation and bulk water supply should not cause the Project Company to unduly prioritize energy production over the other water uses. In the case of transboundary water infrastructure, these challenges may be further compounded by the challenges of potentially competing national views on how to operate the asset, including upstream versus downstream priorities, as well as an increase in the number of stakeholders involved.

The latter also relates to the question of who will ultimately own the asset after the Project Agreement expires, particularly in transboundary scenarios where multiple countries may have worked together through a PPP to realize the infrastructure project. In addition, financing transboundary water infrastructure projects may involve an additional layer of complexity if, for example, multiple currencies are involved as the energy produced is sold in different countries and/or because hard currency financing has been mobilized.

Water infrastructure PPPs have the potential to create substantial value for public agencies by leveraging the creativity of the private sector and the discipline that private financiers can bring, but a well-organized procurement that encourages healthy competitive pressure is also essential to deliver that value.

An example of a multipurpose water infrastructure project that could be implemented as a PPP and shows the potential role that RBOs can play is discussed in box 17.

Box 17. Lesotho-Botswana Water Transfer Scheme

The Lesotho-Botswana Water Transfer Scheme (L-BWTS) is a transboundary water project that aims to increase water supply, not only in Southern Africa, which is already provided with water under the existing Lesotho Highlands Water Project (LHWP), but also to Botswana by conveying water from the Makhaleng River in Lesotho. This will increase climate resilience for Botswana, Lesotho and South Africa, as well as generate electricity via hydropower and a higher irrigation potential. Climate resilience has become particularly relevant following severe droughts in the area; the project is designed to bring increased regional water security. The main sponsor is the Orange-Senqu Commission (ORASECOM) on behalf of member states: Lesotho, Namibia and South Africa.

The project is estimated to cost P15-20 billion (US$ 1.3–1.7 billion) in capital expenditure and P450 million (US$ 39 million) in annual operating expenditure. According to a desktop study conducted on behalf of the Republic of Botswana, a PPP structure may be considered. Given the size of the project, funding and financing would likely come from a range of sources, including government and IFIs. If pursued as a PPP, private financing would also be part of the solution. As of 2021, ORASECOM is undertaking studies to better understand the scope, the route, and the long-term economic implications of the project. These studies, especially outstanding feasibility studies, are being funded by the World Bank (with a US$ 2 million grant funding for a first desk study on the scheme), the African Water Facility, the NEPAD Infrastructure Project Preparation Facility Special Fund (with a € 2.1 million contribution for a broad overall technical feasibility assessment), as well as technical assistance contributions from the Global Water Partnership Southern Africa and others.

As is typical for multipurpose water projects, the project will have to navigate competing interests and priorities, which are further complicated by the transboundary nature of this project. For example, Lesotho will likely look to maximize hydropower production, whereas Botswana will focus on long-term drinking water supply and irrigation. Although this could potentially result in conflict and competition over resource allocation, the fact that ORASECOM is leading this effort is an important sign that member states are seeking to collaborate on these issues. Furthermore, ORASECOM can serve as a platform on which to resolve these competing goals. This is even more the case as ORASECOM also includes Namibia, the most downstream state, which although will not benefit directly from the project will need to be kept informed and consulted.

Source: CRIDF, 2018

Financing instruments in public-private partnerships (PPPs)

In many PPPs, private debt and equity are used to finance the required capital investment. Debt and equity each have their own risk and return profile, with debt being compensated through interest payments and equity through dividends to shareholders. Private debt and equity may also be combined with public funding and financing in what is often referred to as "blended finance".

To attract private financing, investment guarantees and insurance can help mitigate some of the political risks and make the overall risk profile more palatable to potential investors. As these guarantees are used to cover private investment, the Project Company and its investors are responsible for obtaining and paying for them. The Multilateral Investment Guarantee Agency (MIGA), part of the World Bank Group, can guarantee up to 90% of a cross border private equity investment and 95% of private debt principal against non-commercial risks. For example, MIGA guarantees coverage that includes transfer restriction (including inconvertibility), expropriation, war and civil disturbance, breach of contract, and non-compliance of financial obligations. MIGA charges an annual fee for the guarantee, normally expressed as a small percentage of the loan amount. Other IFIs often require a counter-guarantee from the host government when issuing guarantees, but MIGA guarantees do not require a counter-guarantee but they do need approval by the host country. This type of guarantee can minimize the political risk exposure for debt and equity investors as it provides recourse against potential government interference and/or disputes between investors and governments, which is particularly relevant for emerging markets. As a result, investors can be shielded from risks they cannot manage well, while still being wholly responsible for technical and commercial risks.

The following section will discuss private equity and debt for infrastructure PPP projects in more detail, followed by an introduction to the concept of blended finance in section 2.3, accompanied by several case studies illustrating how private and public funding and financing have been harnessed for transboundary water infrastructure projects.

Equity

In infrastructure PPPs, equity investors effectively play the role of owner, although formal ownership of the asset is typical retained by a public entity. Equity investors are given the right to operate the asset and earn a return on their investment in the form of dividends over a predefined period. Once this period has elapsed, the asset is handed back to the public agency, typically free of charge. Equity can come from a variety of sources, including domestic and international entrepreneurs and/or companies, infrastructure development funds, and international financial institutions with both a private sector mandate and the ability to invest equity, such as the International Finance Corporation (IFC), a member of the World Bank Group.

These equity investors control the Project Company of the infrastructure asset. The Project Agreement defines the rights and responsibilities of the Project Company and the public entity. These typically include the performance requirements and the payment mechanism to be used. The latter defines how the Project Company is compensated for its investment as well as what deductions may be imposed if the Project Company cannot meet the performance requirements and other obligations. If the project is well-structured, equity investors will be the first to absorb losses from cost overruns, poor performance, or lower than expected revenues that cannot be recovered from subcontractors. This "first loss" attribute is a key benefit of equity as it serves to incentivize the Project Company, controlled by the equity investors, to deliver the project on time and on budget while adhering to the performance requirements.

Although equity is typically substantially more expensive than both private and public debt in terms of its target return, using equity in the PPP financing structure is often seen as essential to achieving a material risk transfer from the public entity to the Project Company. This contractual design limits the public entity's exposure to construction, operating and financing risks as well as cost overruns. Depending on the specifics of the project, equity investors may make a healthy return on their investments; however, they could also lose their entire investment in capital. The non-recourse/limited-recourse nature of project finance typically ensures that investors cannot lose more than their original investment. Given the inherent uncertainty of the risks and returns, in combination with the potential to lose the entire investment, the cost of equity capital is often substantially higher than the debt. This higher cost reflects the risk profile, or rather the perceived risk profile, that equity investors are exposed to. These risks include project specific risks as well as country and regional risks.

Debt

Although the main benefit of using equity in a PPP financing structure is the substantial risk transfer from the public entity to the Project Company, as discussed above, its higher cost of capital negatively impacts the overall project cost. As a result, equity is often combined with private debt to reduce the overall cost of capital while still achieving a material level of risk transfer. Additional benefits of private debt include the extensive due diligence that lenders conduct on the project before agreeing to lend money, as well as the discipline they impose on the Project Company over the life of the project. Public debt typically lacks the same level of due diligence and discipline, as repayment of public debt is often unrelated to the project's revenues and instead is backed by tax revenues.

A key project finance structuring challenge is to determine the appropriate debt-to-equity ratio. This concept is also referred to as "gearing" or "leverage". As private debt is usually cheaper than equity, using more debt will reduce the overall cost of capital and therefore the cost of the project. However, lenders have a limited upside (their best-case scenario is to get fully repaid on time), and although equity investors could potentially see substantial monetary gains (but still at greater risk of losing their entire investment), there are strict limitations on the amount of debt that debt financiers are willing to provide for a given project. As previously discussed on target equity returns, these limitations depend on the types of risks to which lenders are exposed. For example, if the project is exposed to demand risk, lenders may require at least 25% equity, whereas that could be reduced to only 15% if no demand risk is present.

Besides the gearing requirement, the interest rate of private debt is also a reflection of the risk to which lenders are exposed. This means certain geographies or infrastructure sectors that are perceived as riskier will tend to see higher interest rates. In extreme cases, lenders may be unwilling to lend money to certain projects altogether if they believe their risk exposure is too high. In addition, inflation expectations also impact the interest rate as financiers expect to make a positive return after adjusting for inflation. As discussed earlier, guarantees and political risk insurance can help de-risk projects, which should result in more attractive financing conditions and potentially lower interest rates.

> **Loans vs. bonds.** A key difference between a bond and a loan is that a bond is highly tradeable. If you buy a bond, there is usually a market where you can trade bonds. Another key difference is that loans are negotiated directly between the lender (often a bank) and the borrower. The limited number of parties involved allows the loan to be more easily tailored to the borrower's needs compared to bonds.

Private debt can be split into bank loans and bonds. Bank loans can come from a variety of sources including domestic commercial banks, international commercial banks and international financial institutions with private sector mandates, such as the IFC, FMO and Proparco. Regarding the latter group, it is important to distinguish financiers from development banks that lend directly to governments, as the financing conditions are likely substantially different. Public lending to governments is often concessional with tax revenues used to repay such debt. In the case of lending to a Project Company by, for example, the IFC, the repayment of that debt is based solely on project revenues, typically with no recourse to tax revenues or other government funds. Those debt instruments tend to be priced in a way that is intended to be similar to the rates available from commercial banks, which are likely substantially higher than the interest rate on public debt.

In addition to bank financing, private debt can be raised through a bond issuance or private placements. A bond issuance refers to the sale of debt securities through a public offering. A private placement is similar but limits the offering to a small number of selected debt financiers, such as pension funds and insurance companies. One of the advantages of a private placement compared to a public bond issuance is reduced disclosure requirements, which can be costly and time consuming. Note that private bond financing is less common as an infrastructure financing solution outside of the United States.

2.2.3　Innovative financing initiatives

In recent years, impact investing has become more prominent. Impact investments are investments made with the intention to generate a positive, measurable social and environmental impact alongside a financial return. Impact investments can be made in both emerging and developed markets and target a range of returns from below market to market rate, depending on investors' strategic goals. In the context of impact investing, a number of specialty bonds have emerged, including green bonds and social impact bonds. These bonds are types of private placements where the proceeds are used for pre-specified types of projects with high environmental or social impact potential. They are also sometimes referred to as "use of proceed bonds". For green bonds, these projects are climate and/or environmentally based. The World Bank issues its own green bonds that are used to "raise funds from fixed income investors to support World Bank lending for eligible projects that seek to mitigate climate change or help affected people adapt to it" (World Bank, 2013). The World Bank has issued over US$13 billion in green bonds; each is trade triple-A quality, as with other World Bank bonds.

For social impact bonds, these projects support net positive social outcomes; this type of bond can also be called pay-for-success financing. It serves to cover upfront costs for socially relevant service interventions. Social impact bonds also function to reduce the government's role in welfare provision; they allow social investors to take on the risks associated with innovative or experimental service delivery methods. The social impact bonds "pay market rate of return if predefined outcome targets are met" (Warner, 2013). By accepting this kind of repayment conditionality, investors are effectively accepting a below market risk-adjusted financial return as they also account for the value of the social benefits in their investment decision process.

Despite the fact that the universe for green bonds and for social impact bond investors is growing, competition from other environmental or social initiatives may make it challenging for RBOs to take advantage of them. Furthermore, the (conditional) repayment obligation of bonds means that the RBO still needs a revenue stream to service the debt, similar to more traditional forms of debt. A new concept that has been generating interest among water sector practitioners are Blue Peace Bonds (Box 18).

Box 18. Blue Peace Bonds

New conceptual frameworks for alternative and innovative funding and financing of basin management and development have emerged in recent years, although most remain largely at the conceptual stage. One of these potential innovations is Blue Peace Financing, an initiative promoted by the Swiss Agency for Development and Cooperation (SDC) together with various other government, academic, international and civil society partners, such as Geneva Water Hub and the United Nations Capital Development Fund (UNCDF).

The Blue Peace initiative envisages the development of a multisectoral and transboundary master plan compromised of investment plans that cover infrastructure needs as well as data, monitoring and other soft assets. All the countries in the basin would then share ownership of the master plan, which would provide a basis for long-term cooperation to the benefit of all sectors and countries, while reducing conflict risk and increasing stability and peace.

To finance the projects in the master plans, the Blue Peace Financing concept envisages the use of Blue Peace Bonds which aim to blend public and private instruments into a single, lower risk instrument. In this case, the public funds are used to attract additional public and private financing in order to meet the project's overall financing needs, presumably in the form of credit guarantees or grants, not dissimilar to blended finance (see section 2.3). Rather than public bonds issued by riparian countries, these bonds would be issued by transboundary water organizations or municipalities and repaid using the cash flows of the underlying projects, not dissimilar to the PPP project finance approach (see section 2.2). Surplus cash flows from one project could potentially be used to support other projects that lack a robust revenue stream. The Blue Peace Bonds would be marketed to both domestic and international investors.

One of the challenges that Blue Peace Financing is trying to overcome is the costly and time-consuming process of negotiating financing terms between the issuer, banks and governments, which would simplify the process of raising financing for project implementation. In addition to requiring a legal basis that allows transboundary water organizations or municipalities to issue debt to finance infrastructure projects, a critical success factor for this innovative approach will be strong political leadership from the riparian countries to support such an initiative.

UNCDF, the main implementing agency of the Blue Peace initiative, is in the process of rolling out a Blue Peace pilot project in collaboration with OMVS and OMVG. As of early 2021, the implementation phase for OMVG is ongoing and the technical assistance process for the development of OMVG's basin wide master plan has already begun. The second part of the Technical Assistance will include the design of the financial structure based on the results of the master plan, and it will provide support to OMVG during the process of issuing the financial instrument on the capital market. Although still in the early implementation stage, it will be interesting for practitioners to follow how the Blue Peace Financing pilot unfolds to assess how it could be adapted to other RBOs.

Source: Blue Peace, 2018, interview with UNCDF staff

As previous sections have demonstrated, there are many different types of private debt that could potentially be leveraged to finance PPP transboundary water infrastructure projects. When combined with equity, an optimal financing solution can be created that ensures material risk transfers from the public entity to private financiers. However, in practice, PPP projects often also incorporate public funds and/or financing, as explored in section 2.3 on blended finance.

Another innovative approach to leveraging financial resources is the establishment of endowment funds. These funds are established by foundations or similar actors, with financial resources provided through donations from which withdrawals can be made over a longer period of time for specific (typically not-for-profit) purposes. Up to now, there are no such endowment funds in place for shared basins. However, interesting ideas and concepts have been developed that merit further exploration, including the fully independent hybrid Cubango-Okavango Endowment Fund (Box 19).

Box 19. The Cubango-Okavango Endowment Fund

A recent innovative financing instrument – an endowment fund – was developed for the Cubango-Okavango River Basin (CORB). The aim of the fund is to provide long-term financing for projects related to livelihood improvement and environmental conservation across the basin. The structure combines two types of funds: a sinking fund and an endowment fund, with the ultimate objective to enable consistent withdrawals from invested capital for financing basin projects.

The sinking fund aims to collect +US$ 20 million coming from bilateral and multi-lateral development organizations, as well as the three riparian states: Angola, Botswana and Namibia. The endowment fund aims to generate US$ 250 million from individuals, foundations, corporations and impact investors. Once the investment target has been reached, the fund will commence investments in livelihoods and ecosystem interventions.

The fund is set up in form of an independent Company Limited by Guaranteed in Botswana. Its institutional structure comprises three management levels: i) the highest decision-making body of five members, including one from each riparian state, one non-government livelihoods anchor and one non-government ecosystem anchor; ii) seven board directors, one from each riparian state, and four independent, non-government experts, who will meet quarterly to oversee the business and affairs of the company, and to ensure that the fund delivers on its purpose; iii) one executive officer employed by the board of directors who is responsible for administrative activities and operational efficiency.

Source: http://cridf.net/RC/wp-content/uploads/2019/10/P3669_CORB_4_pager_WEB_ARTWORK.pdf

2.3 Blended financing

Blended financing refers to the strategic use of development finance for the mobilization of additional finance towards sustainable development in developing countries. By combining public funding and financing with specific instruments, commercial financiers can overcome risks that they cannot easily absorb. In addition, the blended finance approach can mobilize private debt and equity financing that may otherwise not have been available. An additional rationale for blending public and private capital is that both come with their distinct advantages and disadvantages, which can potentially be overcome – at least partially – when combined. More specifically, private financing tends to be expensive as it compensates investors for the risks they take on, whereas public financing lacks that same level of risk transfer and is often substantially cheaper than private financing as repayment is typically not linked to the project itself. If structured intelligently, governments can use public funding/grants as well as lower cost public financing to cover part of a PPP project's capital costs while still ensuring material risk transfer through the use of private financing for the remainder of the project cost. Where appropriate, risk mitigation instruments such as guarantees and insurance products can be used to lower the cost of private capital and/or overcome barriers to private financing. The overall cost of capital under this approach will be lower compared to a financing solution that only uses private capital. In addition, public funds can potentially be used as a backstop to protect the Project Company against specific downside scenarios, which can help improve private financing conditions, reducing the overall project cost. Given the large capital needs for most transboundary water infrastructure PPP projects, many projects do in fact combine public and private financing, although the term "blended" finance may not have always been used.

> **Blended finance:** OECD (2018) defines blended finance as the strategic use of development finance for the mobilization of additional finance towards sustainable development in developing countries. Key instruments that can help mitigate certain risks for private financiers, and thus mobilize commercial debt and equity, include guarantees and insurance products, currency hedges, first loss capital, viability gap funding and technical assistance.

Box 20. Congo Basin Blue Fund

Although not described as "blended finance" by its promoters, the proposed structure of the Congo Basin Blue Fund appears to contain some similarities with blended finance. The Congo Basin Blue Fund is a mechanism aimed at helping countries in the Congo River Basin to finance water-related activities (e.g. navigation, hydropower, irrigation, fisheries and tourism) that are expected to mitigate climate change in the region, and thus boost their economies while fostering cooperation and peace between them. The vision is to establish a fund with annual contributions of €100 million that would be used to pay interest on loans from IFIs as well as to cover the costs of insurance and other technical charges. As such, the Congo Basin Blue Fund would use its grant funding to potentially help lower the cost of capital for transboundary infrastructure projects. Among suggested contributors to the fund are the GCF and GEF, as well as states, IFIs and private donors. The fund would be managed by a governing board, including representatives of governments, regional organizations and IFIs. The fund is aimed at becoming operational by the 26th UN Climate Change Conference of the Parties (COP26), scheduled in November 2021.

Source: https://brazzavillefoundation.org/images/nos-actions/congo-basin-blue-fund.pdf
Exchanges with the Chief Executive of the Brazzaville Foundation

---

The case studies presented below illustrate different ways to harness public and private funding and financing in a PPP structure for transboundary water infrastructure projects.

2.3.1 Bujagali Hydropower Project – Uganda

The Bujagali Project is a 250 megawatt (MW) run-of-the-river hydroelectric power plant on the Nile River in Uganda with an adequate reservoir for daily storage, an intake powerhouse complex, and a rock filled dam with a maximum height of about 30 metres. The project was commissioned in 2012 and sells electricity to the local utility provider under a 30-year power purchase agreement (PPA). Evacuation of electricity from the project site required the construction of about 100 kilometres of transmission line, as well as the construction of a substation. The transmission line is part of a transboundary high voltage power line linking the Bujagali Dam in Uganda to a substation in Lessos, Kenya. The line connects the electricity grids of the two countries and is promoted by the Nile Equatorial Lakes Subsidiary Action Program (NELSAP), part of the NBI, as an energy sharing initiative.

Map 3. The Bujagali Hydropower Project in Uganda

Potential for complications arose due to the project's location. The dam sits at the crossroads of the Lake Victoria basin and the Nile basin. In the Lake Victoria basin, Uganda lies downstream of Kenya and Tanzania; in the Nile basin, Uganda lies upstream and shares the basin with nine other countries including Sudan and Egypt. The riparian states of Lake Victoria – less affected by the project – expressed minimal desire for involvement, whereas the Nile basin states – more affected by the project – were initially uneasy with regard to how this might impact flow rates into their own territory. As Uganda lies within the two basins and is both exposed upstream and downstream, Uganda may potentially have been seen as more credible in acting towards basin interests and also perceived to better incorporate lower basin states' concerns.

In addition, the project's main purpose as a power generator helped circumvent potential transboundary conflict. Technical studies had found that the run-of-the-river hydropower plant would have no significant impact on water flow. This allayed the concerns of the downstream countries on the Nile in that their water flows would not be impacted. Egypt sent a letter to Uganda stating that it did not object to the project. As a result, the project was able to move forward.

The next challenge came in the form of capital requirements. The project was developed as a PPP to maximize the benefits of private investment while also leveraging public financing. The overall project cost was US$ 866 million, with a debt-to-equity ratio of 78:22. A Project Company, Bujagali Energy Limited (BEL), was formed to develop the project. Sponsors of BEL include Sithe Global Power (58%), Industrial Promotion Services of Kenya (31.5%) and the Government of Uganda (10.5%). By involving downstream basin members, such as Kenya, the Project Company could represent multiple basin interests. The engineering, procurement and construction (EPC) contract was a fixed price turnkey contract between BEL and Salini Costruttori of Italy and Alstom Power, one of its key subcontractors. The turnkey EPC contract required the EPC contractor to meet BEL's 44-month construction schedule, with delays resulting in the payment of penalties to BEL.

For BEL and its commercial lenders, broad World Bank Group participation was critical to mitigating the other risks associated with the provision of long-term financing for a transboundary hydropower project in sub-Saharan Africa. World Bank Group participation included:

- World Bank: US$ 115 million Partial Risk Guarantee (PRG) to protect commercial lenders, with guaranteed risks including government failure to fulfil payment obligations relating to purchasing of energy and outstanding termination payments, political force majeure events, changes in law (making contractual agreements unenforceable), and currency convertibility or transferability.

- IFC: UP to US$ 130 million in loans.

- MIGA: Up to US$ 120.3 million in guarantees to protect against political risk.

- International Development Association (IDA): US$ 80 million general budget support, and US$ 13.5 million in technical assistance.

The involvement of the World Bank Group provided risk mitigation and assurances to commercial banks and other lenders. EIB, AfDB, Proparco, AFD, DEG, KfW, FMO and commercial banks (Absa Capital, Standard Chartered Bank) joined the project under the PRG. The transmission line to export power from the project was financed by AfDB and Japan International Cooperation Agency (JICA). Bujagali represented a major achievement in project financing given the risks involved with a large hydropower project in sub-Saharan Africa. Moreover, despite the complications inherent to large transboundary infrastructure, the project gained acceptance from riparian states and successfully applied for several types of both public and private financing and funding, highlighting the success of a blended finance approach.

Figure 6. Financing Structure of Bujagali Hydropower Project

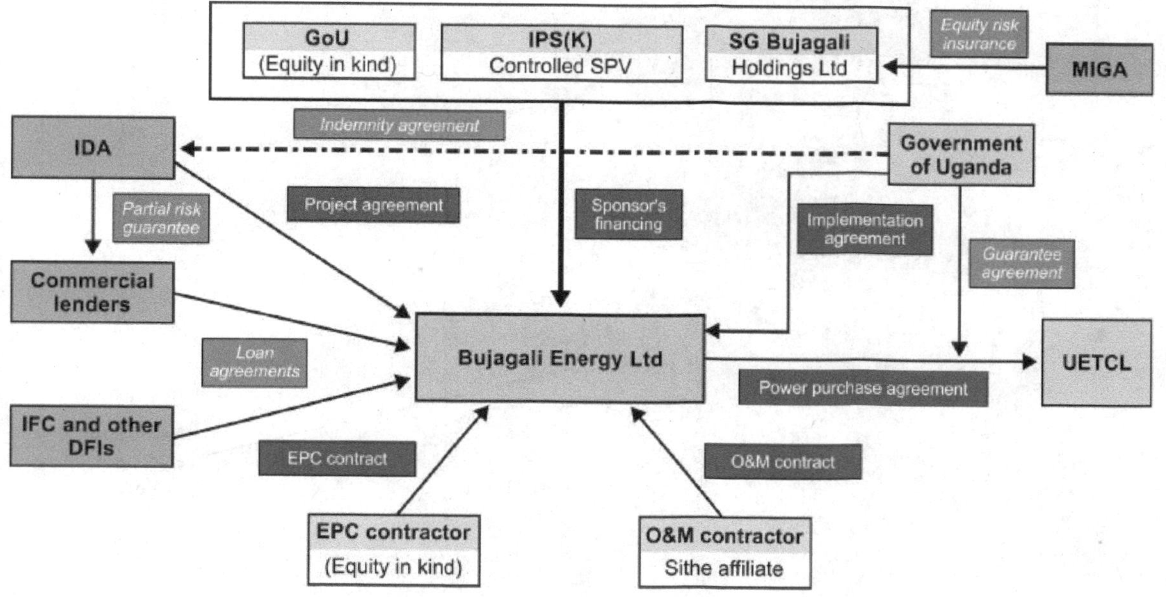

Source: World Bank

The financial closure of the project demonstrated the private sector's willingness to invest in a large complex transaction, which was made possible only after extensive power sector reforms had taken place. This was catalyzed by the role played by the World Bank in providing risk mitigation and a contractual framework underlying the bankability of the project for the private sector.

2.3.2 Nam Theun 2 Hydropower Project – Lao PDR

The Nam Theun 2 Hydropower Project (NT2) is a transboundary and transbasin diversion power plant on the Nam Theun River in Lao PDR that was commissioned in 2010 (though plans date back to the 1920s when it was first identified as a suitable location for a hydropower project). The Nam Theun River, part of the Mekong River, is a tributary to the Xe Bang Fai River. This interconnectedness further complicated the stakeholder environment as the project impacted not only its immediate basin but also the Mekong River from where it flowed and drained into the Xe Bang Fai River. Although located in Lao PDR, the basin extends into Thailand.

These complications meant that the US\$ 1.45 billion multipurpose project spent over a decade under construction, after having spent nearly a decade in the project preparation phase. Commercial export of electricity from the plant to Thailand finally began in March 2010. The project has an installed capacity of 1,070 MW and generates 6,000 gigawatt hours (GWh) of power a year. A substantial part of the plant's capacity (995 MW) is used to produce electricity for export to the Electricity Generating Authority of Thailand as part of a long-term PPA signed in 2003. In addition, the project will use the remaining 75 MW to supply electricity to the state-owned Électricité du Laos. For both Thailand and Lao PDR, the production of electricity has been hugely beneficial, providing a major incentive for the basin states to work together to achieve optimal results.

Operated by Nam Theun 2 Power Company (NTPC), the PPP project has a concession period of 31 years, including a 25-year operating period. NTPC is owned by a consortium including the Électricité de France International (EDF) (at 35%), the Electricity Generating Public Company Limited of Thailand (at 25%), Italian-Thai Development of Thailand (at 15%), and the Government of Lao PDR (at 25%). It therefore represents a typical PPP structure with the involvement of both public and private entities/companies as well as the government of the host state. At the end of the operating period, after it has delivered the benefits for all involved partners, both public and private, the project will be transferred to the Government of Lao PDR.

Map 4. The Nam Theun 2 Hydropower project in Lao PDR

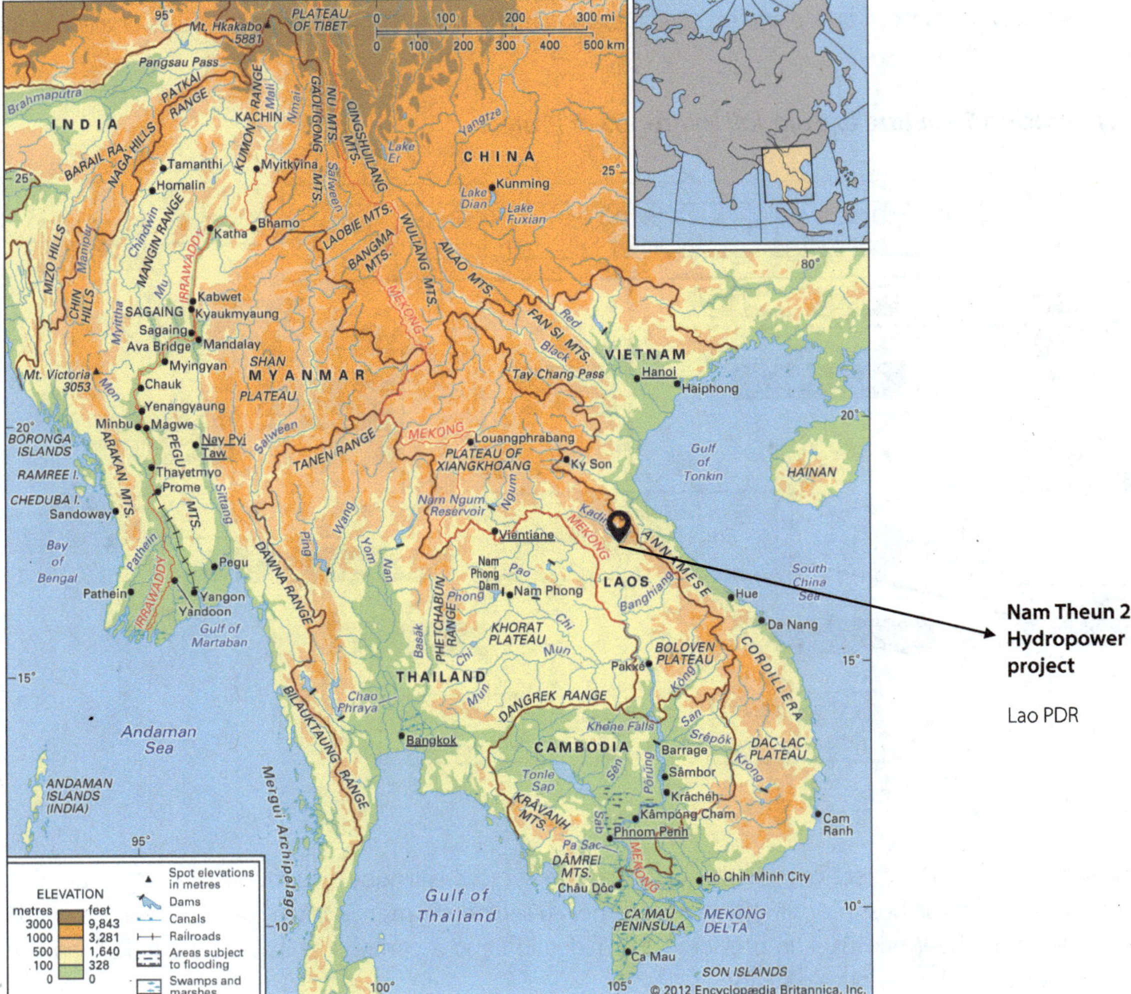

Source: Encyclopaedia Britannica.
Disclaimer: The boundaries and names shown and the designations used on this map do not imply official endorsement or acceptance by the United Nations © United Nations Economic Commission for Europe (2020)

The shared transboundary ownership of the NTPC helped involve diverse stakeholders, representing both Laotian and Thai interests. Using a mixture of public and private debt as well as equity under a PPP structure, the project successfully raised the necessary capital despite a (perceived) high cross-border risk. Key to this success were the grants and loans provided by various international financing institutions including:

- World Bank Group: US$ 20 million IDA grant to the Lao PDR Government for environmental and social expenditures, and for the government to purchase equity in the project company; US$ 91 million MIGA guarantee to cover political risk; and a US$ 50 million IDA partial risk guarantee.

- ADB: US$ 70 million loan and US$ 50 million guarantee to cover political risk.

- Grants given by IDA and the Agence Française de Développement (AFD).

The involvement of the international financing institutions and export credit agencies provided risk mitigation and assurances to nine international commercial banks and seven Thai commercial banks.

Given its transboundary nature and the involvement of a myriad of international financial actors, debt was issued in both hard currency (US dollars, 64%) and local currency (Thai baht, 36%). Equity was also sold in both currencies, although the amount of equity purchased with Thai baht was substantially lower than with US dollars.

CHAPTER 3 CHALLENGES AND OPPORTUNITIES IN FUNDING AND FINANCING TRANSBOUNDARY WATER COOPERATION AND BASIN DEVELOPMENT

This chapter summarizes the key findings of the publication and specifically focuses on the challenges and opportunities related to specific funding and financing resources. It outlines the way ahead for improving the financial sustainability of water resources cooperation and management as well as basin development.

3.1 Key findings on costs of shared water cooperation, management and development

The needs for financial resources for cooperation as well as the management and development of shared water resources in transboundary basins are manifold and often perceived as relatively high. Member states' commitment and related financial contributions to transboundary water cooperation and basin development are also of great importance.

The costs relating to the establishment and maintenance – and the effective functioning – of joint bodies vary considerably across the world's basins. This depends largely on the scope and the focus of joint bodies – itself influenced by factors such as the technical capacity of member states and the mandate of the joint body. The costs for managing and developing shared water resources vary even more – again, depending on the mandate and the functions of a joint body (or the commitments to cooperation made by riparian states with no joint bodies). It is important to note once again that the costs borne directly by member states of a joint body, through the national implementation of jointly agreed upon activities, typically do not feature in basin budgets and are therefore difficult to calculate.

Joint bodies often experience an expansion of their mandate and functions over time. A periodic review of the extent of their mandate, and therefore the activities they implement, is still required to help joint bodies direct their limited resources to the water management challenges of greatest importance in a basin. In this way, they can address key water management and basin issues, while meeting the needs of the member states.

At the same time, it should be noted that although the costs of both institutionalized cooperation and joint basin management and development may appear high in absolute numbers, they are generally quite low compared to the benefits that cooperation joint management and development can provide and given the overall budget of riparian countries, even for developing countries with limited financial capacity. In the Mekong River Basin, for instance, the contribution of member states to the MRC is currently set at around US$ 2 million per country per year. Compared to the overall size of the economy (approximately US$ 18 billion for Lao PDR in 2018) or government budgets (US$ 3.9 billion for Lao PDR in 2019), and given the huge importance of the Mekong River for the basin countries, this amount does not appear to be unreasonable. It is often a case of prioritizing government spending, as well as the importance afforded to basin cooperation, management and development that matters.

Since the benefits of transboundary water cooperation are often not sufficiently clear and tangible, it may be useful to identify and communicate such efforts, for example, by using the benefits assessment methodology developed by UNECE (2015)[9] or other approaches to identify, assess and possibly quantify the benefits for all parties involved.

3.2   *Key challenges and opportunities of the different funding and financing sources*

Identifying and acquiring a source of funding and financing for cooperation over shared water resources and for their management and development has been a challenge in many basins around the world. The key source of funding of any type of water cooperation, management and development, whether at the national or transboundary level, tends to be public funding in the form of direct government contributions. With water resources management being a public good, government funding continues to play (or at least should play) a crucial role.

However, in many regions around the world, direct government funding for transboundary water management and basin development has been insufficient. The COVID-19 pandemic and the ensuing economic recession and socioeconomic decline have only worsened the situation, bringing millions of people into poverty and at times turning the attention of policymakers towards other pressing issues. This has led to cuts in member states financial contributions to several basin organizations. Various other financial sources have therefore been used or at least explored in the past. This should, however, not distract from the fact that the operation of key functions of transboundary water management is still a public task and it is therefore unlikely to generate interest from private financiers. This requires that riparian governments in shared basins financially commit to the management and development of their river basins; a task that might potentially be easier in the context of national budget negotiations if the benefits of cooperation are clear to all the parties involved, including those beyond the water sector, for example, the Ministry of Finance, Ministry of Economic Planning, and so on.

Beyond direct government funding of transboundary water management and development, this publication has examined numerous other types of public and some private funding and financing sources. One key takeaway is that there is no single obvious replacement for direct government funding, at least when it comes to covering the core costs and project, programme and activity costs of transboundary water cooperation. Although different funding models have been tried across various RBOs and countries, each come with their advantages and disadvantages, but no obvious "winning strategy" has emerged. As RBOs and riparian countries struggle to meet the funding needs of transboundary water cooperation and basin development, many have suggested that the private sector can offer relief. This publication shows that private capital, by and large, is only available for projects that are able to generate a return for its financial investors. By their very nature, the operational activities of RBOs do not typically generate revenues, let alone profits, even though their work can have important social, environmental and economic impacts on the basin and its riparian states. In this context, private capital can, and should, play a role in transboundary water cooperation and particularly transboundary basin development, but this will likely remain limited to infrastructure projects where there is a clear path for private sector financiers to make a fair risk-adjusted return on their investment.

Even though there is no hidden pot of money available, this chapter provides RBOs and riparian states with a comprehensive overview of potential funding sources that they could consider. Table 2 summarizes these different funding and financing sources, highlighting their respective challenges and opportunities from the perspective of RBOs and riparian states.

---

9   Policy Guidance Note on the Benefits of Transboundary Water Cooperation: Identification, Assessment and Communication (UNECE publication, 2015). Available at https://unece.org/environment-policy/publications/policy-guidance-note-benefits-transboundary-water-cooperation.

Trees along Syr Darya river, Kazhakstan

Table 2. Opportunities and challenges of funding and financing sources

		Opportunities	Challenges	Use	Example
PUBLIC SOURCES	Direct Member State Contribution	• Reflects the "public good" function of water management • Demonstrates member states' commitment to institutionalized cooperation and multisectoral joint basin development • Ensures financial self-sustainability and independence from external funds • Can have numerous benefits for riparian states committing to cooperation, incl. peace, regional cooperation and integration, etc.	• Needs strong legal, institutional and procedural linkages between basin level cooperation, national planning, and management and budgeting • Can create budget competition against other national priorities • Can be unreliable year to year depending on national budgets • Cost-sharing decision-making can be arduous and fraught with conflict	• Core costs • Project, programme and activity costs	Most joint bodies Section 2.1.1
	Regional Taxes	• Can offer relative stability in year to year funding amounts and allows for more effective, future-looking planning • Overcomes weaknesses in national budgets and limits competition against other national priorities • Can help equalize influence between member states with unbalanced budgetary means • Reflects regional nature and integrated approach to shared basins	• Taxes are disconnected from the transboundary water activities, thus potentially reducing involvement and interest of national governments • RBOs typically have limited influence over budget allocation and cannot set the tax rate • Membership of regional body and RBO may not fully overlap, potentially creating tensions about ownership and contributions • Creates dependence on other regional bodies and vulnerability to changes within them	• Core costs • Project, programme and activity costs	CICOS Section 2.1.2
	User and Polluter Fees	• Reflects the actual use and responsibilities of water resources • Prevents the externalization of costs by individual users/user groups at the expense of the entire riparian community • Large industrial water users/polluters may have significant financial means to contribute	• Difficult to establish at transboundary level given the different national regulations on usage and polluter fees • High transaction costs (i.e. cost of collection), especially for small-scale users/polluters • Potentially challenging to demonstrate added value of transboundary water collaboration to water end users, thus limiting willingness to pay • Mispricing of polluter fees can have unintended side effects (excessive pollution or stifling of economic activity) • So far, no successful example of application at transboundary level available	• Core costs • Project, programme and activity costs	None at transboundary level Section 2.1.3

	Opportunities	Challenges	Use	Example
Sale of Data and Services	• New approach to funding that monetizes joint bodies' products • Can help popularize the work of RBOs, providing an opportunity for greater recognition among the broader public	• Not expected to generate significant funding • May distract from work of the joint body on key water management issues to more revenue-generating activities	• Immaterial	MRC, CICOS Section 2.1.4
Management and Administration Fees	• A potentially effective way to get donors/ partners to cover some of the RBO's operating costs • Adds a layer of accountability to donors/ partners	• Depends on the RBO's mandate (management and administration fees not applicable to coordination-oriented RBOs) • Depends on willingness of donor/partner policies to pay, which may decline over time • Associated fee may not cover full staff costs • May redirect staff hours away from the main aims of the RBO/key water management issues	• Project, programme and activity costs	MRC Section 2.1.5
Project Management Fees	• Can give RBOs greater visibility when involved in the preparation of potentially large infrastructure projects • Adds a layer of accountability to owners/ financiers • Provides substantial learning opportunities for staff	• Depends on the RBO's mandate (project management fees only applicable to RBOs with an infrastructure implementation mandate) • Associated fee may not cover full staff/other costs • Staff must have necessary (and potentially highly specialized) skill sets	• Infrastructure development	NBI Section 2.1.6
Public Loans	• Often offer below market interest rates • Repayment likely not tied to financed activity but instead backed by national tax revenues	• Eligibility for loans depends on RBO's legal status • Repayment obligation plus accumulated interest • Currency fluctuations if loan is in hard currency • Can come with extensive conditionality	• Project, programme and activity costs • Infrastructure development	OMVS Section 2.1.7

	Opportunities	Challenges	Use	Example
Public Grants	• "Free money," no repayment requirement	• Dependent on the RBO's mandate (only applicable to RBOs with a project implementation mandate) • May come with "strings attached" • May not align with RBO's strategic plans • Project specific and typically cannot be applied to day-to-day operations	• Project, programme and activity costs • Infrastructure development	Many joint bodies Section 2.1.8
Technical Assistance	• Can help kick-start cooperation with both technical and financial capacity • Leverage external expertise and lessons learnt elsewhere	• Can potentially affect ownership of basin cooperation and management • Can create dependencies on external resources (technical, financial, etc.)	• Core costs • Project, programme and activity costs	Many joint bodies Section 2.1.9
Climate Funds	• Innovative funding source with potentially high amounts available	• Long and tedious application procedures that sometimes surpass the capacity of joint bodies • Legal arrangements and requirements are not always clear • Limited successful examples so far • Can only be used for specifically climate-related activities and not for other basin management and development measures	• Climate-related project, programme and activity costs • Climate-related Infrastructure development	OSS LVBC NBA VBA Section 2.1.10
Private Grants and Donations	• "Free money," no repayment requirement	• May come with "strings attached" • May not align with RBO's strategic plans • Project specific and typically cannot be applied to day-to-day operations • Rare as philanthropy tends to prioritize contributions to NGOs with hands-on project implementation over government-led transboundary water cooperation	• Project, programme and activity costs	Section 2.2

		Opportunities	Challenges	Use	Example
PRIVAT SOURCES	Private Equity	• Through the PPP structure, equity investors are fully incentivized to help a project succeed • More material risk transfer to private sector than under traditional (non-PPP) project structure	• Part of PPP project structure, which is expensive and resource-intensive to procure and set up • Equity investors to earn a positive risk-adjusted return so project must generate sufficient revenue • Equity is more expensive compared to public and private debt as equity investors are taking more risk	• Transboundary water infrastructure development	Bujagali and Nam Theun 2 Sections 2.3.1 and 2.3.2
	Private Debt (loans, bonds)	• Through the PPP structure, lenders are fully incentivized to help a project succeed • More material risk transfer to private sector than under traditional (non-PPP) project structure • Private lenders add additional layer of due diligence and market discipline • Using private debt reduces cost of capital compared to an equity-only financing solution	• Part of PPP project structure, which is expensive and resource-intensive to procure and set up • Lenders expect to be fully repaid (including interest) so project must generate sufficient revenue • Private debt is more expensive compared to public debt as lenders in a PPP are taking more risk	• Transboundary water infrastructure development	Bujagali and Nam Theun 2 Sections 2.3.1 and 2.3.2
	Innovative Financing	• Tap into private financing sources with potentially lower return expectations as investors seek modest return in combination with social/environmental impact • Potentially give access to debt financing solutions for RBOs that currently cannot borrow	• Largely untested for transboundary water cooperation • Financiers expect to make a social/environmental impact-adjusted fair return so project must still generate sufficient revenue	• Project, programme and activity costs • Transboundary water infrastructure development	OMVS OMVG
	Blended Financing	• Leverage grants to reduce project cost • Leverage public debt to reduce overall cost of capital • Leverage private debt and equity, in combination with grants and public debt, to create a relatively low-cost financing structure that mimics the comprehensive risk transfer of a well-structured PPP	• Complex to put together blended financing solution, requiring substantial resources	• Transboundary water infrastructure development	Bujagali and Nam Theun 2 Sections 2.3.1 and 2.3.2

Indus river in Himalayas, India

CONCLUSION AND TAKEAWAYS

This section summarizes the key findings of the publication with a focus on the financial needs for transboundary water cooperation and basin development as well as the various sources of funding and financing that is potentially available to meet those needs. Based on the analyses and the different examples examined, these key takeaways can also provide basin managers, policymakers and representatives of the public and private financial sector important insights to help strengthen their joint efforts to ensure the sustainable funding and financing of transboundary water cooperation and basin development for the benefit of the world's shared basins and their riparian communities.

Highlight the benefits of transboundary water cooperation and basin development, and build a strong legal and institutional framework are the crucial steps for states and joint bodies with shared basins to mobilize financial resources

1. **Transboundary water resources management and cooperation are crucial to preventing and mitigating conflict over shared water resources**. In addition, they can fuel development and economic growth in member states as well as improve "quality of life" indicators. Transboundary water resources management and cooperation can thus provide benefits in the form of win-win solutions that the unilateral use of shared water resources cannot achieve on its own, which is also the reason why transboundary water resources management and cooperation is included in the SDGs. Inability to access needed funding and financing for transboundary water resources management and cooperation in many basins therefore implies that the potential benefits of transboundary basin cooperation and development are not fully realized.

2. **Different types of financial resources are needed for different stages of the cooperation and basin development process**. Financial resources are required in order to: collect and process the data and information required to manage water resources in the basin; launch and sustain the process of transboundary cooperation and its institutional arrangements; and implement investments and other basin management and development measures.

3. **International basin treaties and arrangements, joint bodies and specifically RBOs provide the legal and institutional framework for transboundary water resources management and cooperation, and are crucial for creating an enabling environment to raise funding or financing.** These legal and institutional frameworks are unique and reflect the vision of their member states. They serve as the basis for generating and sharing the benefits of cooperation over time, across riparian states, and between users. Effective agreements and strong RBOs are also enabling factors to attract and mobilize the financial resources needed for transboundary water cooperation and management. In some cases, financial arrangements between contracting parties are included in the legal framework.

4. **River basin management plans and investment plans play an essential role in joint bodies' efforts to encourage transboundary water cooperation, including across sectors through a nexus approach, and to advance basin development.** They are also an important instrument for communicating the benefits of cooperation to member states and to help attract additional financial resources. Implementing these plans typically requires substantial efforts and investment, although certain activities and investments may also be carried out at the national level.

Despite some challenges, domestic budgetary resources from riparian states is and should be the primary financial source to support joint bodies and basin activities

5. **Member states are typically the main contributor to joint bodies' budgets, especially, but not solely, for core costs.** This is a logical consequence given the common perception of water management as a public responsibility. The status of RBOs as intergovernmental organizations reinforces this idea as they are created and maintained by contracting states. Besides their contributions to RBO budgets, member states often mobilize financial resources outside the joint body/basin framework for activities implemented at the national level which also contribute to transboundary water management and cooperation.

6. **Joint bodies often struggle to get funding from member states for programme costs, core costs as well as transboundary projects as they compete with many other national priorities for budget allocations, challenging their ability to realize the full potential benefits of cooperation.** Core costs and activity costs can weigh heavily on member state budgets in some regions of the world, even though their total contribution is typically small compared to overall government expenditure. Stronger engagement with national and local development planning and budgeting processes is needed to ensure that sufficient budgetary resources are allocated to joint bodies.

7. **Joint bodies should better communicate the benefit of their work to their member states and all relevant actors within them.** To the extent possible, RBOs should attempt to quantify benefits derived from their work or use qualitative assessments to help individual ministries of finance and other ministries in charge of planning to better understand the societal impact of transboundary cooperation, thereby strengthening the case for larger budget allocations.

8. **The cost sharing of a joint body among riparian states (equal cost sharing versus key-based cost sharing) must be carefully balanced between the principle of sovereign equality on the one hand and their potentially unequal economic capacities on the other.** Budgets and cost-sharing mechanisms can change as challenges in the basin or a state's financial capacities evolve over time. However, cost-sharing mechanisms should always aim to reflect a commitment to cooperation from all the states involved, often reflected in the principle of equality.

9. **As principal funders of transboundary cooperation, riparian states should define and express their expectations with regard to a joint body's work and activities, reviewing and monitoring their activities regularly.** Since the RBO's budget comes largely from member state contributions, and therefore ultimately from individual taxpayers, member states should ensure that these resources are spent efficiently and effectively while meeting their collective needs. Explicit demands, clear expectations, and effective monitoring of the activities of joint bodies and their outcomes are important elements.

Other public financing and funding resources offer opportunities for diversifying financial sources for riparian states and joint bodies

10. **While the international community often plays a key role in launching and supporting transboundary initiatives, strong local buy-in and ownership is essential for longevity and sustainability.** Strong commitments by countries expressed through domestic funding of transboundary cooperation can facilitate access to international funds or support, which often comes in the form of grants, loans and technical assistance. Requiring that member states provide funding for operating costs, even in the startup years of joint bodies, in return for donor support for specific activities or purchases can help ensure local ownership. Without member state funding, projects are likely to be unsustainable once external support dries up. Strategies for achieving financial self-sustainability are therefore an important element of long-term planning.

11. **There is no silver bullet or a hidden pot of gold to cover the shortfalls in transboundary cooperation funding; however, alternatives and/or complements to traditional member state contributions do exist with some proving to be more promising than others.** There is no such thing as "free money"; all funding and financing mechanisms discussed in this publication come with strings attached in one form or another. Even grants may come with certain conditions or requirements. As such, RBOs and member states must be wise in allocating efforts to search for funding opportunities that closely align with the RBO's overall mandate and plans.

12. **Different funding and financing sources are required at different stages of river basin management and development as well as during the different stages of individual projects.** Early project development will require financial means other than those for infrastructure construction or later operations and maintenance. Accordingly, member states, donors, financiers and others have the opportunity to contribute at different stages in a way that best aligns with the needs of the basin (and individual projects), as well as their own priorities.

13. **Additional public funding and financing mechanisms do exist to complement and complete member states contributions, with some showing more promise than others.**

    Regional tax: A limited number of RBOs successfully used taxes collected by regional organizations to fund a variety of initiatives, but there are no known examples in which a tax was created for the sole purpose of funding a RBO.

    User/polluter fees: While user/polluter fees mechanisms appear to be in line with the principles of integrated water resources management and have been studied for potential transboundary implementation, there are no known examples in which user/polluter fees are actually used to fund RBOs or transboundary water resources management.

    Sale of data/services: The sale of data or services tends to have a very low revenue potential overall. Some joint bodies have mobilized management fees, administration fees and project administration fees, but these effectively require donors or project sponsors to cover a part of a joint body's operating expenses, thus raising questions about sustainability.

    Loans: Joint bodies may be able to attract loans to implement certain activities or projects. In practice, many RBOs face challenges in securing loans as they may not have the legal status that would allow them to take on loans and/or they lack a revenue stream that could be used to repay the loan. As such, it is more likely that national governments, rather than the RBO, will apply for loans and make the funds available to the RBO. Given that repayment is required, loans may be more appropriate for revenue generating activities or projects, although countries can decide to use loan proceeds to fund non-revenue generating transboundary infrastructure or activities.

    Grants: Joint bodies may also be able to attract grants to implement certain activities or projects. Although grants do not require repayment, they typically come with limitations on how the money is used. For example, grant proceeds are often used to implement specific projects or activities and often cannot be used for the RBO's day-to-day operational expenses, depending on the grant design and related conditions.

Climate funds: Climate funds is a special category of grants that could potentially fund certain activities related to climate change adaptation and mitigation carried out by joint bodies, although there are few examples to date of RBOs successfully applying for such funds.

Technical assistance: Technical assistance provides a way for joint bodies to acquire funding for capacity-building and specific projects, but it also comes with certain requirements and is not a permanent solution.

Private funding and financing offer potential opportunities to cover transboundary basin infrastructures development costs

14. **There are very few examples of private funding without the expectation of repayment being used for transboundary water resources management.** Although some examples of philanthropic funding of joint bodies activities do exist, these are exceedingly rare and have not been found outside of North America.

15. **Private financing also has a role to play but is typically limited to revenue generating activities or projects.** As private capital seeks a return on investment, deploying private capital tends to be limited to infrastructure projects with robust revenue generating potential, as is the case, for example, with hydropower projects. Even though private capital can also be employed for non-revenue generating projects, this would require another revenue stream to repay private financiers. In environments with strong governance and high capacity, this revenue stream could come from the government. However, this is less common in emerging markets. The return requirement on private capital limits its applicability to ongoing operations of joint bodies, which typically do not generate revenues.

16. **Public-private partnerships (PPPs) have been instrumental in leveraging private capital for transboundary water infrastructure projects.** Under a PPP structure, the private financier takes responsibility for the design, construction, financing, operations and maintenance of a public infrastructure project, while earning a return on that investment. The public agency typically retains formal ownership of the project throughout its life but regains operational responsibilities once the asset is handed back at the end of the project term, typically free of charge. A well-structured PPP can help mobilize private capital in the form of debt and equity while also transferring the substantial risk from the government to the private party.

17. **Transboundary water infrastructure projects are endowed with risks given the complexity of a multi-actor environment, but there are risk mitigation instruments to overcome them.** These complexities are compounded in emerging markets where governance, economic strength, and stability may be in short supply. As such, private financiers may be hesitant to get involved if too much of the risk is placed on their shoulders. However, credit guarantees, political risk insurance, and other instruments can be used to overcome some of these issues, helping mobilize private capital for transboundary water infrastructure projects. Cooperative arrangements, whereby several basin states share the cost and risks through joint management and development, may be another way to help mitigate risks.

18. **Blended finance refers to the use of public funding and financing in conjunction with private financing, which has been used to develop water infrastructure projects across the globe.** If structured intelligently, governments can use public funding/grants as well as lower the cost of public financing to cover part of a project's capital costs while still ensuring material risk transfer through the use of private financing for the remainder of the project cost. Many PPPs around the world have effectively employed the concept of blended finance, even though it may not have always been called that.

19. **Innovative financial instruments are being developed and tested, which could potentially lead to new solutions to finance transboundary water cooperation and development.** Recent financial innovations include green bonds and social impact bonds. The former is to be used exclusively for projects with a climate or environmental focus whereas the latter links repayment to

the achievement of certain predefined social goals. Both types of instruments have a repayment expectation, meaning that they are more appropriate for revenue generating projects. In addition, increasing competition from other environmental or social initiatives may make it challenging for RBOs to take advantage of the growing market interest in these innovative financial products. Another ongoing innovation are Blue Peace Bonds. A key challenge that the Blue Peace initiative is trying to overcome is the costly and time-consuming process of negotiating financing terms between the issuer, banks and governments, as this would simplify the process of raising financing for project implementation. Nevertheless, the practical implications are still being worked out, especially as public sources are being used for technical assistance and de-risking in a blended finance scenario. In this regard, the Blue Peace Bonds are also an example of blended finance (see box 18).

20. **There is a continued need for further capacity-building and exchange of experiences as well as information about funding and financing opportunities, challenges and lessons learned.** The platform of the Water Convention[10] (serviced by UNECE), among others, provides an opportunity for such capacity-building and exchange. Facilitating financing of transboundary water cooperation and basin development[11] will remain in the Water Convention's work programme for years to come.

---

[10] https://www.unece.org/env/water/

[11] https://www.unece.org/environmental-policy/conventions/water/areas-of-work-of-the-convention/financing-of-transboundary-water-cooperation.html

Rhône Glacier, source of the Rhône, Switzerland

REFERENCES

ABN (2010). Etude Stratégique sur le Financement Autonome et Durable des Activités de l'ABN. BRL Ingénierie/ICEA, January 2010 [In French].

Artiga, Raúl (2003). The Case of the Trifinio Plan in the Upper Lempa: Opportunities and challenges for the shared management of Central American transnational basins. Paris: UNESCO PC-CP Series. Available at https://unesdoc.unesco.org/ark:/48223/pf0000133304

Blue Peace (2018). Blue Peace: Invest in Peace Through Water. https://blue-peace-movement.github.io/website/Invest_in_Peace_through_Water.pdf

Blue Peace Movement. Financing and Investing in Blue Peace. https://www.thebluepeace.org/blue-peace-financing Accessed on 20 July 2021.

BMU (2010). Wasserwirtschaft in Deutschland. Grundlagen, Belastungen, Maßnahmen. Dessau-Roßlau, BMU/UBA (Hrsg.) [In German].

CBLT (2010). Étude Stratégique sur le financement autonome et durable des Activités de la CBLT. N'Djamena: Commission du Bassin du Lac Tchad (unpublished internal document). [In French].

CICOS (2016). Schéma Directeur d'Aménagement et de Gestion des Eaux de la CICOS (SDAGE). Kinshasa: Commission Internationale du Bassin Congo-Oubangui-Sangha [In French].

CICOS (2015). Etude sur les Mécanismes de Financement de la Commission Internationale du Bassin Congo-Oubangui-Sangha. Kinshasa: CICOS/GIZ/RebelGroup (confidential) [In French].

Congo Basin Blue Fund (no year). Congo Basin Blue Fund. Brazzaville Foundation for Peace and Conservation. Available at https://brazzavillefoundation.org/images/nos-actions/congo-basin-blue-fund.pdf

CRIDF (2018). Lesotho-Botswana Water Transfer (L-BWT) Scheme. The Orange-Senqu River Commission (ORASECOM). Available at http://www.orasecom.org/_system/writable/DMSStorage/2711P2953_project_pitches_LBWT_web_FINAL.pdf

Earth Security Partnerships (2018). The Finance Sector's Contribution to Water and Peace. Risk management policies and impact investments to support transboundary water cooperation. Available at https://earthsecuritygroup.com/wp-content/uploads/2018/12/ESP-Finance-Water-Peace.pdf

European Investment Bank. Red Sea Dead Sea Water PPP Phase 1. https://www.eib.org/en/projects/loans/all/20150559 Accessed on 20 July 2021.

EUWI (2013). Mapping of Financial Support to Transboundary Water Cooperation in Africa. EU Water Initiative Africa Working Group, May 2013.

GCF (2020). Adapting to Climate Change in Lake Victoria Basin. Green Climate Fund. https://www.adaptation-fund.org/project/adapting-climate-change-lake-victoria-basin-burundi-kenya-rwanda-tanzania-uganda/ Accessed on 20 July 2021.

GIZ (2020a). Niger Flussbehörde (ABN). Support for the Niger Basin Authority. https://www.giz.de/projektdaten/projects.action?request_locale=en_EN&pn=201225143 Accessed on 20 July 2021.

GIZ (2020b). Conserving biodiversity in the Nile Basin transboundary wetlands. https://www.giz.de/en/worldwide/43317.html Accessed on 20 July 2021.

Global High Level Panel on Water and Peace (2017): *A Matter of Survival*, Geneva. Available at https://www.genevawaterhub.org/sites/default/files/atoms/files/a_matter_of_survival_www.pdf

GTZ (2007). Donor activity in transboundary water cooperation in Africa. Results of a G8-initiated survey 2004-2007. Eschborn: Federal Ministry for Economic Cooperation and Development.

Henkel, Marianne, Fiona Schüler, Alexander Carius, Aaron T. Wolf (2014). Financial Sustainability of International River Basin Organizations. Eschborn: Federal Ministry for Economic Cooperation and Development.

HLPW (2018). Making every drop count. An Agenda for Water Action High-Level Panel on Water Outcome Report. UN and World Bank. Available at https://sustainabledevelopment.un.org/content/documents/17825HLPW_Outcome.pdf

IKI (2020). Biodiversity conservation and utilisation of ecosystem services in wetlands of transboundary significance in the Nile Basin. International Climate Initiative. https://www.international-climate-initiative.com/en/details/project/biodiversity-conservation-and-utilisation-of-ecosystem-services-in-wetlands-of-transboundary-significance-in-the-nile-basin-15_IV_045-427?iki_lang=en Accessed on 20 July 2021.

IMG Rebel (2019). Étude sur la Réforme Institutionnelle de la CICOS. Rapport d'analyse final. Washington, DC: IMG Rebel, September 2019 (internal CICOS document) [In French].

IRENA (2012). Renewable Energy Technologies: Cost Analysis Series – Hydropower. Volume 1: Power Sector. Bonn: International Renewable Energy Agency. Available at https://www.irena.org/-/media/Files/IRENA/Agency/Publication/2012/RE_Technologies_Cost_Analysis-HYDROPOWER.pdf

IUCN, UNECE, SDC and USAID (2020). Sio-Malaba-Malakisi Basin Investment Plan and Financial Sustainability Strategy. Available at https://www.iucn.org/sites/dev/files/content/documents/smm_policy_brief_-_march_2021.pdf

Kweifio-Okai, Carla. Where did the Indian Ocean tsunami aid money go? *The Guardian*, 25 December 2014. https://www.theguardian.com/global-development/2014/dec/25/where-did-indian-ocean-tsunami-aid-money-go

LVBC (2019). Experiences on Climate Change Adaptation in Transboundary Basins. Presentation at the 4th Meeting of the Global Network of Basins Working on Climate Change Adaptation, 14-15 February 2019, Geneva. Lake Victoria Basin Commission.

MRC (2000). New Formula for Member Annual Contributions, adopted at the 7th Meeting of the MRC Council, 24 October 2000, Pakse, Lao PDF. Mekong River Commission (confidential document).

MRC (2019a). *Review of the Decentralization of Core River Basin Management Function Activities. Undertaken for the Mekong River Commission as part of the Mid-Term review of the Strategic Plan 2016-2020*, Vientiane: MRC Secretariat, 22 February 2019

MRC (2019b). *Sustainable Financing of Transboundary Water Cooperation in Basins – Case of the MRC*, presented at the 2019 Stockholm World Water Week, 28 August 2019

MRC (2016). *Integrated Water Resources Management-based Basin Development Strategy 2016-2020 for the Lower Mekong Basin*, Vientiane: MRC Secretariat, https://www.mrcmekong.org/assets/Publications/strategies-workprog/MRC-BDP-strategy-complete-final-02.16.pdf

MRC (2014). Final draft report for comment: Core River Basin Management Functions Decentralisation Project, Financial Component. Towards Financial Sustainability of the Mekong River Commission through Member Countries' Contributions, Vientiane: Mekong River Commission (unpublished internal document).

MRC Data Portal. Data fees for MRC Data Portal price categories. https://portal.mrcmekong.org/about/data-fees Accessed on 20 July 2021.

Mukherji, Anuradha (2019). Funding Flows: Transboundary Considerations of Disaster Recovery. Available at https://doi.org/10.1093/acrefore/9780199389407.013.223

NBA (2009). Étude stratégique sur le financement autonome et durable des activités de l'ABN. Rapport Final, Novembre 2009, Niamey, Niger: Niger Basin Authority [In French].

NBI (2020). Commissioning of Rwanda-Uganda Power Interconnection and Synchronization of Kenya-Uganda-Rwanda-Burundi-DRC Grids in 2020. NELSAP-CU, 09 March 2020. Nile Basin Initiative. https://nilebasin.org/nelsap/index.php/en/news-events/311-commissioning-of-rwanda-uganda-power-interconnection-and-synchronization-of-kenya-uganda-rwanda-burundi-drc-grids-in-2020

NBI (2012). NBI Financing Strategy. Entebbe, Uganda: Nile Basin Initiative. (unpublished internal document, March 2012).

NBI (2011a). Briefing Paper. For consideration by the Nile Council of Ministers for future NBI Member State contributions to the Nile Secretariat, November 2011. Entebbe, Uganda: Nile Basin Initiative.

NBI (2011b). Institutional Development Study. Financial Sustainability. Entebbe, Uganda: Nile Basin Initiative (unpublished internal document).

Nolden, Tim (2020). Financing Public River Basin Management Functions in the Elbe and the Meuse River Basin, IHE Delft Master of Science Thesis, 25 March 2020.

ODI (2002). Financing Transboundary Water Management, Water Policy Brief No 2, July 2002. London: Oversees Development Institute.

OECD (2019). Making Blended Finance Work for Water and Sanitation, Unlocking Commercial Finance for SDG 6. Paris: Organisation for Economic Co-operation and Development. Available at http://www.oecd.org/environment/resources/making-blended-finance-work-for-sdg-6-5efc8950-en.htm

OECD (2018). Financing Water. Investing in sustainable growth. Policy Perspectives. OECD Environment Policy Paper No 11. Paris: Organisation for Economic Co-operation and Development. Available at https://www.oecd.org/water/Policy-Paper-Financing-Water-Investing-in-Sustainable-Growth.pdf

ORASECOM (2009). Feasibility Study for the Development of a Mechanism to Mobilize Funds for Catchment Conservation. Business Case for the ORASECOM Conservation Fund. Centurion, South Africa: Orange-Senqu River Basin Commission (unpublished internal document, June 2009).

Rees, Judith A., James Winpenny and Alan W. Hall (2008). Water financing and governance. TEC Background Papers No. 12. Stockholm: Global Water Partnership, Technical Committee (TEC).

Republic of Botswana Ministry of Minerals, Energy and Water Resources (2018). Lesotho Highlands Botswana Water Transfer Desktop Study – Final Report.

Robotti, Chiara (2017). New Life for the Dead Sea, *European Investment Bank,* 19 September 2017. https://www.eib.org/en/stories/red-sea

Rozenberg, Julie and Marianne Fay, eds. (2019). Beyond the Gap. How Countries Can Afford the Infrastructure They Need while Protecting the Planet. Sustainable Infrastructure Series. Washington, DC: World Bank Group.

SADC (2010). Guidelines for Strengthening River Basin Organizations. Funding and Financing, Gaborone, Botswana: Southern African Development Community, Water Division/GIZ. Available at https://www.sadc.int/files/4513/5333/8265/SADC_guideline_establishment.pdf

Schmeier, Susanne (2021). *Managing river basins across governance levels – The complexity of legal and institutional frameworks.* Ferrier, B. and Jenkins, A. (eds.). Handbook of Catchment Management. Hoboken: Wiley.

Schmeier, Susanne (2013). *Governing international watercourses. River Basin Organizations and the Sustainable Governance of Internationally Shared Rivers and Lakes.* London/New York: Routledge.

SIWI (2020). Public-Private Partnerships and the risk of corruption in the water sector. Stockholm International Water Institute. Available at https://www.siwi.org/wp-content/uploads/2020/03/Water-Integrity-in-Water-Infrastructure_2020.pdf

South Pole (2020). An Investor Guide on Basin Water Security Engagement: Aligning with SDG 6, Zurich: Swiss Federal Office for the Environment. Available at https://www.southpole.com/uploads/media/an-investor-guide-basin-water-security-engagement.pdf

UNCDF (2019). Blended Finance in the Least Developed Countries. United Nations Capital Development Fund. Available at https://www.uncdf.org/en/article/4220/blended-finance-in-ldcs-report

UNDP-GEF (2016). International Waters – Delivering Results. New York: UNDP Bureau of Policy and Programme Support. New York: United Nations Development Programme and the Global Environment Facility.

UNECE (2021). A revised draft People-first Public-Private Partnerships Evaluation Methodology for the Sustainable Development Goals (ECE/CECI/WP/PPP/2020/3/Rev.1). Available at https://unece.org/sites/default/files/2021-05/2014920E_0.pdf

UNECE (2018). Background document High-Level Workshop on Financing Transboundary Basin Development, Astana, Kazakhstan, 9 October 2018. Available at https://www.unece.org/fileadmin/DAM/env/documents/2018/WAT/10Oct_9_HLWS_Astana/Final_Background_Document_Workshop_on_FinancingTBCoop_15_11_2018.pdf

UNECE/UNESCO/UN-Water (2021). Progress on Transboundary Water Cooperation. Global baseline for SDG indicator 6.5.2, Geneva: UNECE, UNESCO, UN-Water, https://www.unwater.org/publications/progress-on-transboundary-water-cooperation-652-2021-update/

USAID/CAREC (2020). Handbook Establishment and Operation of Small Basin Councils in Central Asia and Afghanistan. Almaty, Kazakhstan: The Regional Environment Centre for Central Asia. Available at http://www.riverbp.net/upload/iblock/1a4/1a4469ef7e26714ff483b3083efb1017.pdf

Warner, Mildred (2013). Private finance for public goods: Social impact bonds. *Journal of Economic Policy* Reform. no. 16, vol. 4, pp. 303–319. DOI: 10.1080/17487870.2013.835727

Water Funder Initiative. Priority Strategies. https://www.waterfunder.org/priority-strategies

World Bank (2019). Financing Climate Change Adaptation in Transboundary Basins: Preparing Bankable Projects. Washington, DC: International Bank for Reconstruction and Development / The World Bank. Available at https://unece.org/sites/default/files/2020-12/Financing_Climate_Adaptation_Final_Paper_pub.pdf

World Bank (2018). Promoting Development in Shared River Basins. Case Studies from International Experience. Washington, DC: International Bank for Reconstruction and Development / The World Bank. Available at https://openknowledge.worldbank.org/bitstream/handle/10986/29449/W17105.pdf?sequence=4&is%20Allowed

World Bank. Rwanda, Tanzania and Burundi – Regional Rusumo Falls Hydroelectric Project. *Loans & Credits*, 6 August 2013. https://www.worldbank.org/en/news/loans-credits/2013/08/06/rwanda-tanzania-and-burundi-regional-rusumo-falls-hydroelectric-project Accessed on 20 July 2021.

World Bank. World Bank Approves Rusumo Falls Hydropower Plant. *Press release,* 6 August 2013. https://www.worldbank.org/en/news/press-release/2013/08/06/world-bank-approves-rusumo-falls-hydropower-plant Accessed on 20 July 2021.

World Water Council (2015). Water: Fit for Finance? Catalyzing National Growth Through Investment in Water Security. Marseille: World Water Council. Available at https://www.worldwatercouncil.org/sites/default/files/2017-10/WWC_OECD_Water-fit-to-finance_Report.pdf

Yu, Winston (2008). Benefit Sharing in International Rivers: Findings from the Senegal River Basin, the Columbia River Basin, and the Lesotho Highlands Water Project. World Bank: Africa Region Water Resources Unit Working Paper No. 1. Washington, DC: The World Bank.

Zingraff-Hamed, Aude, Barbara Schröter, Simon Schaub, Robert Lepenies, Ulf Stein, Frank Hüesker, Claus Meyer, Christian Schleyer, Susanne Schmeier and Martin P. Pusch (2020). Perceptions of Bottlenecks in the Implementation of the European Water Framework Directive. *Water Alternatives*, vol. 13, no. 3, pp. 458–483.